COME UP HIGHER
&
LOVE YOUR LIFE

Transformational Bible based Daily Devotional Planner

Rhonda D. Dennis

BALBOA.PRESS
A DIVISION OF HAY HOUSE

Balboa Press books may be ordered through booksellers or by contacting:

Balboa Press
A Division of Hay House
1663 Liberty Drive
Bloomington, IN 47403
www.balboapress.com
844-682-1282

Print information available on the last page.

ISBN: 979-8-7652-4681-8 (sc)
ISBN: 979-8-7652-4680-1 (e)

Balboa Press rev. date: 11/20/2023

Dear Reader,

This planner is a one year, step-by-step, journey to becoming and achieving more of what God wants for you, enabling you to Come Up Higher & Love Your Life!

Jammed packed with transformational information! Including an opportunity to create a Biblically Sound Daily routine, enabling you to grow in six areas of life: Spiritually, Mentally, Emotionally, Physically, Relationally, and Financially!

Start your day with a **Morning Readiness Routine** that helps you prepare you for whatever encounter(s) the day brings. As you incorporate **Daily Practices** into your **Personal Development**, you will...

Grow Spiritually, as you learn to include God, in your everyday activities, pray, put on his armor, affirm your relationship with him and who you are - with him in your life! *But grow in the grace, and in the knowledge of our Lord and Savior Jesus Christ. To him be the glory both now and forever. Amen. 2 Peter 3:18*

Gain Clarity, about life's difficulties, as you navigate worldly thinking vs. God's word, memorize verses, and declare, affirmations over your life. *Then you will know the truth, and the truth will set you free. John 8:32*

Gain Peace, as you focus on gratitude, your new routine and what you are learning, verses day to day problems. *Set your mind on things above, not on earthly things. Colossians 3:2*

Create Better Relationships, with yourself and others, as you learn to recognize your personal triggers, practice self-love techniques, communication skills, work through mindfulness questions - bringing new awareness and stirring up life-changing transformation!

> *Jesus said, 'Love the Lord your God with all your heart and with all your soul and with all your mind.' And the second is like it; 'Thou shalt love thy neighbor as thyself.' Mathew 22:37,39*

Get Healthy and/or **Lose Weight** and **Get Physically fit,** as you start practicing self-care, eating from the wholesome foods list, and working out to a program you create – incorporating good habits and replacing bad ones! *...you were bought with a price. Therefore, honor God with your bodies. 1 Corinthians 6:20*

Become Financially Secure, by prioritizing living expenses, tithing/charitable contributions, savings, spending, and paying off debt. *Dishonest money dwindles away, but whoever gathers money little by little makes it grow. Proverbs 13:11*

Gain Success in your endeavors, as you set intentions, to prioritize what you do with your time – working within God's will for your life. *Be very careful, then. How you live – not as unwise but as wise, making the most of every opportunity, because the days are evil. Ephesians 5:15-16*

All this and more! As you embark on this journey, I invite you to join the **private** Facebook group, **Come Up Higher Group**. Where you can ask questions and share experiences, workout videos, recipes, dances, and much more!

You can also watch for, *Come Up Higher Introductory Workbook*, as a follow up to this planner, encouraging more growth in all six areas of life.

Blessings in all that you do!

Rhonda Dennis October 2023

Whatever you do, work at it with all your heart, as working for the Lord, not for human masters, Colossians 3:23

JANUARY

Birthdays

_____

_____

_____

_____

_____

_____

_____

_____

_____

52 WEEKLY BIBLE STUDY TOPICS

Who is God

Heirs in Christ

Walking out your Salvation

Renewing the Mind

Being anointed

Taking thoughts Captive

Dealing with Difficult People

Self-Control

Appropriate Boundaries

Christ like Qualities

Idols

Blessings

Abundance

Security

Trust

Peace

Grieving

Idols

Blessings

Being a Light

Grace

Stability

Enabling others

Sexual Relations

Made in His image

Disobedience

Branches

Who the enemy is

Getting Baptized

Jesus;' Resurrection

Negativity

Righteousness

Overcoming Fear

Spiritual Battles

How to love

How and When to Pray

Healing

Morality

Service to Others

Necessary Struggles

Gratitude

Spiritual Gifts

Strongholds

Surrendering

Morality

Service to Others

Mercy

Defeating the Enemy

Maturity

Symbols of the Bible

Managing Money

Protecting your Heart

Tree of Life

Fruits & Seeds

Prayer

Our Father in heaven, Hallowed be your name, Your kingdom come your will be done, on Earth as it is in Heaven. Give us today our Daily Bread and Forgive us our debts, as we also have forgiven our debtors. And lead us not into temptation but deliver us from the evil one. *Mathew 6:9-*

Christ-Like Qualities

Loving	Trusting
Courageous	Peaceful
Surrendered	Creative
Compassion	Honest
Mindful	Humble
Accepting	Bold
Considerate	Grateful
Dependable	Confident
Discerning	Curious
Compassion	Patient
Considerate	Kind
Productive	Forgiving
Obedience	Faithful
Perseverant	Discipline
Temperate	Integrity
Authenticity	Courteous
Generous	Respectful
Responsible	Patient
Unchanging	Wise
Righteous	Eternal
Omnipotent	Sovereign

Armor of God

Helmet of SALVATION -NOTHING can separate you from God. *Romans 8:38-39*

Breastplate of RIGHTOUSNESS - ALL your sins are covered; you are purified. *1 John 1:7*

Shield of FAITH - He works ALL things for our good. *Romans 8:28*

Belt of TRUTH - God's word breathes life into your soul. *Hebrews 4:12*

Sword of the SPIRIT, word of God. Speak it OUTLOUD, to defeat the enemy. *Mathew 17:20*

Shoes of PEACE – *Philippians 4:7* and the READINESS to SERVE. *Luke 12:43*

Affirmation

I am a

_____,

_____,

_____

child of God.

*Choose three qualities, from Christ-like Qualities List, you would like to become or improve on. Speak aloud every day. Change anytime.

3

Memory Verse

_____
_____
_____
_____
_____
_____
_____

Slow down....
Check your Choices & Responsibilities

Emotional IQ
Beliefs
Attitude
Intentions
Energy/Mood
Reactions/Responses
Actions/Behaviors
Decisions
Time

My Intention/Goal/Dream

_____
_____
_____
_____
_____
_____
_____
_____
_____
_____

Morning Mindset

1. Who is one person I can lift up/help today?

_____
_____

How?

_____
_____

2. One action, I can take, to-ward MY Intention, Goal, Dream(s) today Is…

_____
_____
_____
_____

3. What is the cost if I do not take the action(s)?

_____
_____
_____
_____

4. What can I intentionally learn today to support myself?

_____
_____
_____
_____

5. What area of growth am I focusing on this week?

_____
_____
_____
_____

Anti-Aging Face Regimen

<u>Morning</u>
Wash face w/cleanser
Vitamin C Serum
Hyaluronic Acid
Sunscreen SPF15

<u>Noon</u>
Sunscreen SPF15
Hyaluronic Acid
Toner (see Recipe)

<u>B4 Bed</u>
Wash Face
Alpha Hydroxy Acid
Retinol
Hyaluronic Acid
*Try a moisturizer w/
hyaluronic acid.

Toner Recipe

Harvest/Purchase
a handful of
Cell Rejuvenating Herb
(Lavender or Rose)
Place into 12oz. boiling
spring water, and
Let it sit overnight.
Strain and put into
spray bottle.

Breathe & Meditate

Take 5 minutes to Step away from everyone and everything.

Sit quietly. Once you have settled. (Record yourself or someone, in a monotone voice, saying…)

Think of the most serene place, of which you can think. Breathe Deep. In through your nose. Out through your mouth.

In this place, what is the weather like? Think of how it smells.

Think of how it feels.

What do you see?

Imagine Jesus is there.

He walks toward you.

Can you take his hand?

If not, you can follow him. You begin walking together.

As you walk, just breathe.

Now, open your eyes.

*Do this every morning and anytime you need comfort, strength, peace.
** IF you are unable to take Jesus' hand, keep practicing and it will get easier.

3) **Daily Gratitude's**

_____

_____

_____

Whole Health Cocktail

(drink 4oz. Every Morning)

2T Apple Cider Vinegar
4T Lemon Juice
2c. Cranberry Juice
4c. Water
Follow w/8oz. Bone broth

Raise Your Energy

- Stand and Bounce on your toes every hour.
- Swing your arms in circles
- Take Deep Breaths 10x.
- Brisk 5-minute Walk
- Listen to Uplifting Music
- Take a cold shower
- Take Vitamin B12
- Drink Ginseng tea

Exercise Tips

- Eat protein after working out or strenuous activities.
- Drink water in ounces equal to half your body weight.
- Make sure your sleep is consistent. *Setting your internal clock enables your body in its healing process.
- While working out call an accountability partner.

Fitness Routine

Weight/Height = BMI

Yoga   ____min

Walk   ____min

Aerobics   ____min

Swim   ____min

Cycle   ____min

Hike   ____min

Strength Training

Reps/weight#

Shoulders   ___/___

Arms   ___/___

Abs   ___/___

Chest   ___/___

Legs   ___/___

Buttocks   ___/___

Core   ___/___

*Max heart rate = 220 less Your Age **Low rate = Max multiplied by .65.

Arms – Shoulder pinches and rolls, push-ups, butterflies, Curl ups and Back Rows

Legs – Squats, Step ups, Ball squeezes, Kick backs

Core – Planks and Leg lifts

Cleaning Routine
(See check list in back of book)

Monday
_____
_____
_____

Tuesday
_____
_____
_____

Wednesday
_____
_____
_____

Thursday
_____
_____
_____

Friday
_____
_____
_____

Saturday
_____
_____
_____

Sunday
_____
_____
_____

MUST Do
_____
_____
_____

NEED to Do
_____
_____
_____

WANT to DO
_____
_____
_____

Night Reflections

1. One thing I learned today.

_____

_____

_____

_____

2. What is one thing I can improve on/challenge myself.

_____

_____

_____

_____

_____

3. How am I eliminating distractions? Taking control of my time ...

_____

_____

_____

_____

4. What am I doing to improve my relationships?

_____

_____

_____

_____

5. One question for God today: write it on separate piece of paper, put in a prayer box and leave with it for him.

Sample Routine
(Self Employed)

6:00	Face/Prayer/Armor
6:30	Morning Cocktail & Bone broth
7:00	Breakfast/Bible Study
7:30	
8:00	Bounce & Breathe 10x
8:30	
9:00	Walk 15/Workout 15
9:30	Shower/Ready/ Affirmations
10:00	
10:30	Cleaning (see routine)
11:00	Write
11:30	
12:00	Lunch – Meeting?
12:30	Write
1:00	Emails/Calls/Apt
1:30	
2:00	
2:30	Bounce/Breathe 10min
3:00	Write
3:30	
4:00	Craft/Garden/Visit
4:30	
5:00	
5:30	
6:00	Make Dinner/Go Out
6:30	
7:00	Eat dinner/Watch T.V.
7:30	
8:00	Clean up Dinner
8:30	Walk 15min
9:00	Pamper
9:30	
10:00	Facial/Ready for Bed
10:30	Night Reflections
11:00	Bed

5:00 _____	4:30 _____
5:30_____	5:00 _____
6:00 _____	5:30 _____
6:30 _____	6:00 _____
7:00 _____	6:30 _____
7:30 _____	7:00 _____
8:00 _____	7:30 _____
8:30 _____	8:00 _____
9:00 _____	8:30 _____
9:30 _____	9:00 _____
10:00 _____	9:30 _____
10:30 _____	10:00 _____
11:00 _____	10:30 _____
11:30 _____	11:00 _____
12:00 _____	11:30 _____
12:30 _____	12:00 _____
1:00 _____	12:30 _____
1:30 _____	1:00 _____
2:00 _____	1:30 _____
2:30 _____	2:00 _____
3:00 _____	2:30 _____
3:30 _____	3:00 _____
4:00 _____	

FEBRUARY

Birthdays

_____

_____

_____

_____

_____

_____

_____

_____

_____

DETOX & GET HEALTHY

Whole Body Detox

2 Cucumber

1 Celery Stalk,

½ lemon

1 Hand Spinach

¼ Ginger root
or 1tsp. powder

1 Apple

Gallbladder

Cucumber
Beets
Avocado
Tomatoes
Walnuts

Kidneys

Cranberries
Raspberries
Onion
Olive Oil
Dandelion Root

Eyes

Carrots
Greens
Egg Yolks
Leafy Greens

Liver

Garlic
Grapefruit
Beets
Green Tea
Apples
Barley
Coconut Water
Cruciferous
Veggies
Whole Grains

Bones

Bone Broth
Yogurt
Sardines
Almonds
Lentils
Parsley
Cilantro

Lymph

Asparagus
Strawberries
Sea Veggies
Turmeric
Citrus
Ginger

Pancreas

Blueberries
Garlic
Red Grapes
White Fish
Coconut Oil
Goldenseal

Muscles

Salmon
Lean Beef
Tuna
Shrimp
Chickpeas
Buckwheat

Intestines

Pineapple
Lentils
Oatmeal
Brown Rice
Quinoa
Ginger'

Blood/Heart

Artichokes
Barley
Cherries
Flaxseed
Hemp Seed
Cannellini Beans
Coriander
Cayenne
Curcumin
Rosemary

*Consult physician about food
interactions IF taking Medications.

Prayer

Our Father in heaven, Hallowed be your name, Your kingdom come your will be done, on Earth as it is in Heaven. Give us today our Daily Bread and Forgive us our debts, as we also have forgiven our debtors. And lead us not into temptation but deliver us from the evil one. *Mathew 6:9-*

Christ-Like Qualities

Loving	Trusting
Courageous	Peaceful
Surrendered	Creative
Compassion	Honest
Mindful	Humble
Accepting	Bold
Considerate	Grateful
Dependable	Confident
Discerning	Curious
Compassion	Patient
Considerate	Kind
Productive	Forgiving
Obedience	Faithful
Perseverant	Discipline
Temperate	Integrity
Authenticity	Courteous
Generous	Respectful
Responsible	Patient
Unchanging	Wise
Righteous	Eternal
Omnipotent	Sovereign

Armor of God

Helmet of SALVATION -NOTHING can separate you from God. *Romans 8:38-39*

Breastplate of RIGHTOUSNESS - ALL your sins are covered; you are purified. *1 John 1:7*

Shield of FAITH - He works ALL things for our good. *Romans 8:28*

Belt of TRUTH - God's word breathes life into your soul. *Hebrews 4:12*

Sword of the SPIRIT, word of God. Speak it OUTLOUD, to defeat the enemy. *Mathew 17:20*

Shoes of PEACE – *Philippians 4:7* and the READINESS to SERVE. *Luke 12:43*

Affirmation

I am a

————————————————,

————————————————,

————————————————

child of God.

*Choose three qualities, from Christ-like Qualities List, you would like to become or improve on. Speak aloud every day. Change anytime.

Memory Verse

_____
_____
_____
_____
_____
_____
_____

Slow down....
Check your Choices & Responsibilities

Emotional IQ
Beliefs
Attitude
Intentions
Energy/Mood
Reactions/Responses
Actions/Behaviors
Decisions
Time

My Intention/Goal/Dream

_____
_____
_____
_____
_____
_____
_____
_____
_____

Morning Mindset

1. Who is one person I can lift up/help today?

_____
_____

How?

_____
_____

2. One action, I can take, to-ward MY Intention, Goal, Dream(s) today Is…

_____
_____
_____
_____

3. What is the cost if I do not take the action(s)?

_____
_____
_____
_____

4. What can I intentionally learn today to support myself?

_____
_____
_____

5. What area of growth am I focusing on this week?

_____
_____
_____

Anti-Aging Face Regimen

<u>Morning</u>
Wash face w/cleanser
Vitamin C Serum
Hyaluronic Acid
Sunscreen SPF15

<u>Noon</u>
Sunscreen SPF15
Hyaluronic Acid
Toner (see Recipe)

<u>B4 Bed</u>
Wash Face
Alpha Hydroxy Acid
Retinol
Hyaluronic Acid
*Try a moisturizer w/
hyaluronic acid.

Toner Recipe

Harvest/Purchase
a handful of
Cell Rejuvenating Herb
(Lavender or Rose)
Place into 12oz. boiling
spring water, and
Let it sit overnight.
Strain and put into
spray bottle.

Breathe & Meditate

Take 5 minutes to Step away from everyone and everything.

Sit quietly. Once you have settled. (Record yourself or someone, in a monotone voice, saying…)

Think of the most serene place, of which you can think. Breathe Deep. In through your nose. Out through your mouth.

In this place, what is the weather like? Think of how it smells.

Think of how it feels.

What do you see?

Imagine Jesus is there.

He walks toward you.

Can you take his hand?

If not, you can follow him. You begin walking together.

As you walk, just breathe.

Now, open your eyes.

*Do this every morning and anytime you need comfort, strength, peace.
** IF you are unable to take Jesus' hand, keep practicing and it will get easier.

3) Daily Gratitude's

_____

_____

_____

Whole Health Cocktail
(drink 4oz. Every Morning)

2T Apple Cider Vinegar
4T Lemon Juice
2c. Cranberry Juice
4c. Water
Follow w/8oz. Bone broth

Raise Your Energy

- Stand and Bounce on your toes every hour.
- Swing your arms in circles
- Take Deep Breaths 10x.
- Brisk 5-minute Walk
- Listen to Uplifting Music
- Take a cold shower
- Take Vitamin B12
- Drink Ginseng tea

Exercise Tips

- Eat protein after working out or strenuous activities.
- Drink water in ounces equal to half your body weight.
- Make sure your sleep is consistent. *Setting your internal clock enables your body in its healing process.
- While working out call an accountability partner.

Fitness Routine
Weight/Height = BMI

Yoga	_____min
Walk	_____min
Aerobics	_____min
Swim	_____min
Cycle	_____min
Hike	_____min

Strength Training
Reps/weight#

Shoulders	___/___
Arms	___/___
Abs	___/___
Chest	___/___
Legs	___/___
Buttocks	___/___
Core	___/___

*Max heart rate = 220 less Your Age **Low rate = Max multiplied by .65.

Arms – Shoulder pinches and rolls, push-ups, butterflies, Curl ups and Back Rows

Legs – Squats, Step ups, Ball squeezes, Kick backs

Core – Planks and Leg lifts

Cleaning Routine
(See check list in back of book)

MUST Do

_____

Monday

_____
_____
_____

Tuesday

_____
_____
_____

NEED to Do

_____

Wednesday

_____
_____
_____

Thursday

_____
_____
_____

Friday

_____
_____
_____

WANT to DO

_____

Saturday

_____
_____
_____

Sunday

_____
_____
_____

Night Reflections

1. One thing I learned today.

_____

_____

_____

_____

2. What is one thing I can improve on/challenge myself.

_____

_____

_____

_____

_____

3. How am I eliminating distractions? Taking control of my time …

_____

_____

_____

_____

4. What am I doing to improve my relationships?

_____

_____

_____

_____

5. One question for God today: write it on separate piece of paper, put in a prayer box and leave with it for him.

Sample Routine
(Self Employed)

6:00	Face/Prayer/Armor
6:30	Morning Cocktail & Bone broth
7:00	Breakfast/Bible Study
7:30	
8:00	Bounce & Breathe 10x
8:30	
9:00	Walk 15/Workout 15
9:30	Shower/Ready/Affirmations
10:00	
10:30	Cleaning (see routine)
11:00	Write
11:30	
12:00	Lunch – Meeting?
12:30	Write
1:00	Emails/Calls/Apt
1:30	
2:00	
2:30	Bounce/Breathe 10min
3:00	Write
3:30	
4:00	Craft/Garden/Visit
4:30	
5:00	
5:30	
6:00	Make Dinner/Go Out
6:30	
7:00	Eat dinner/Watch T.V.
7:30	
8:00	Clean up Dinner
8:30	Walk 15min
9:00	Pamper
9:30	
10:00	Facial/Ready for Bed
10:30	Night Reflections
11:00	Bed

5:00 _____	4:30 _____
5:30 _____	5:00 _____
6:00 _____	5:30 _____
6:30 _____	6:00 _____
7:00 _____	6:30 _____
7:30 _____	7:00 _____
8:00 _____	7:30 _____
8:30 _____	8:00 _____
9:00 _____	8:30 _____
9:30 _____	9:00 _____
10:00 _____	9:30 _____
10:30 _____	10:00 _____
11:00 _____	10:30 _____
11:30 _____	11:00 _____
12:00 _____	11:30 _____
12:30 _____	12:00 _____
1:00 _____	12:30 _____
1:30 _____	1:00 _____
2:00 _____	1:30 _____
2:30 _____	2:00 _____
3:00 _____	2:30 _____
3:30 _____	3:00 _____
4:00 _____	

MARCH

Birthdays

_____

_____

_____

_____

_____

_____

_____

_____

VITAMINS/HERBAL SUPPLEMENTS
&What they are for

Heart

L-Leucine
L-Glutamine
Resveratrol
Omega 3-6-9
Quercetin
CoQ10
Hawthorne
Berry
Hibiscus
Panax Ginseng

Brain (40+)

DHEA
PS - Phosphatidylserine
PEA- Phenylethylamine
Magnesium
Melatonin
Rhodiola
Gingko Biloba
Tulsi (Holy Basil)

Whole Body

Multi
B-Complex
Astragalus
Nettles
Red Clover

Muscles

BCAA's
Ashwagandha
Eleuthero
Creatine

Skin

Alpha Lipoic Acid
Hyaluronic Acid
Retinol
Lutein
CoQ10
Collagen
Vit E
DMAE
Squalene

DETOX

L-Glutathione
L-Glucarate
Selenium
Dandelion Root
Burdock
Cascara Sagrada
Milk Thistle

Bones

Vit D3
Vit K2
MSM
Glucosamine
Chondroitin
Comfrey
Lemongrass

Hormones

Saw Palmetto
Damiana
Maca
Fenugreek
Jasmine
Chaste Tree Berry
Black Cohosh

Digestion (GUT)

Probiotic
Prebiotic
Bromelain
Marjoram
Ginger
Aloe

*Research and learn how each is beneficial to your body.
**Alternate your teas.
*** Check with physician IF taking medications

Prayer

Our Father in heaven, Hallowed be your name, Your kingdom come your will be done, on Earth as it is in Heaven. Give us today our Daily Bread and Forgive us our debts, as we also have forgiven our debtors. And lead us not into temptation but deliver us from the evil one. *Mathew 6:9-*

Christ-Like Qualities

Loving	Trusting
Courageous	Peaceful
Surrendered	Creative
Compassion	Honest
Mindful	Humble
Accepting	Bold
Considerate	Grateful
Dependable	Confident
Discerning	Curious
Compassion	Patient
Considerate	Kind
Productive	Forgiving
Obedience	Faithful
Perseverant	Discipline
Temperate	Integrity
Authenticity	Courteous
Generous	Respectful
Responsible	Patient
Unchanging	Wise
Righteous	Eternal
Omnipotent	Sovereign

Armor of God

Helmet of
SALVATION -NOTHING can separate you from God.
Romans 8:38-39

Breastplate of
RIGHTOUSNESS - ALL your sins are covered; you are purified.
1 John 1:7

Shield of FAITH - He works ALL things for our good. *Romans 8:28*

Belt of TRUTH - God's word breathes life into your soul.
Hebrews 4:12

Sword of the SPIRIT, word of God. Speak it OUTLOUD, to defeat the enemy. *Mathew 17:20*

Shoes of PEACE – *Philippians 4:7* and the READINESS to SERVE. *Luke 12:43*

Affirmation

I am a

——————————————,
——————————————,
——————————————
child of God.

*Choose three qualities, from Christ-like Qualities List, you would like to become or improve on. Speak aloud every day. Change anytime.

Memory Verse

_____

_____

_____

_____

_____

_____

_____

Slow down....
Check your Choices & Responsibilities

Emotional IQ
Beliefs
Attitude
Intentions
Energy/Mood
Reactions/Responses
Actions/Behaviors
Decisions
Time

My Intention/Goal/Dream

_____

_____

_____

_____

_____

_____

_____

_____

_____

Morning Mindset

1. Who is one person I can lift up/help today?

_____

_____

How?

_____

_____

2. One action, I can take, to-ward MY Intention, Goal, Dream(s) today Is…

_____

_____

_____

_____

3. What is the cost if I do not take the action(s)?

_____

_____

_____

_____

4. What can I intentionally learn today to support myself?

_____

_____

_____

_____

5. What area of growth am I focusing on this week?

_____

_____

_____

_____

Anti-Aging Face Regimen

<u>Morning</u>
Wash face w/cleanser
Vitamin C Serum
Hyaluronic Acid
Sunscreen SPF15

<u>Noon</u>
Sunscreen SPF15
Hyaluronic Acid
Toner (see Recipe)

<u>B4 Bed</u>
Wash Face
Alpha Hydroxy Acid
Retinol
Hyaluronic Acid
*Try a moisturizer w/
hyaluronic acid.

Toner Recipe

Harvest/Purchase

a handful of

Cell Rejuvenating Herb

(Lavender or Rose)

Place into 12oz. boiling
spring water, and

Let it sit overnight.

Strain and put into

spray bottle.

Breathe & Meditate

Take 5 minutes to Step away from everyone and everything.

Sit quietly. Once you have settled. (Record yourself or someone, in a monotone voice, saying...)

Think of the most serene place, of which you can think. Breathe Deep. In through your nose. Out through your mouth.

In this place, what is the weather like? Think of how it smells.

Think of how it feels.

What do you see?

Imagine Jesus is there.

He walks toward you.

Can you take his hand?

If not, you can follow him. You begin walking together.

As you walk, just breathe.

Now, open your eyes.

*Do this every morning and anytime you need comfort, strength, peace.
** IF you are unable to take Jesus' hand, keep practicing and it will get easier.

3) Daily Gratitude's

_____

_____

_____

Whole Health Cocktail

(drink 4oz. Every Morning)

2T Apple Cider Vinegar
4T Lemon Juice
2c. Cranberry Juice
4c. Water
Follow w/8oz. Bone broth

Raise Your Energy

- Stand and Bounce on your toes every hour.
- Swing your arms in circles
- Take Deep Breaths 10x.
- Brisk 5-minute Walk
- Listen to Uplifting Music
- Take a cold shower
- Take Vitamin B12
- Drink Ginseng tea

Exercise Tips

- Eat protein after working out or strenuous activities.
- Drink water in ounces equal to half your body weight.
- Make sure your sleep is consistent. *Setting your internal clock enables your body in its healing process.
- While working out call an accountability partner.

Fitness Routine

Weight/Height = BMI

Yoga	_____min
Walk	_____min
Aerobics	_____min
Swim	_____min
Cycle	_____min
Hike	_____min

Strength Training

Reps/weight#

Shoulders	___/___
Arms	___/___
Abs	___/___
Chest	___/___
Legs	___/___
Buttocks	___/___
Core	___/___

*Max heart rate = 220 less Your Age **Low rate = Max multiplied by .65.

Arms – Shoulder pinches and rolls, push-ups, butterflies, Curl ups and Back Rows

Legs – Squats, Step ups, Ball squeezes, Kick backs

Core – Planks and Leg lifts

Cleaning Routine

(See check list in back of book)

MUST Do

_____

Monday

_____

_____

_____

_____

Tuesday

_____

_____

_____

_____

NEED to Do

Wednesday

_____

_____

_____

_____

Thursday

_____

_____

_____

_____

Friday

_____

_____

_____

WANT to DO

_____

Saturday

_____

_____

_____

_____

Sunday

_____

_____

_____

_____

Night Reflections

1. One thing I learned today.

_____

_____

_____

_____

2. What is one thing I can improve on/challenge myself.

_____

_____

_____

_____

_____

3. How am I eliminating distractions? Taking control of my time …

_____

_____

_____

_____

4. What am I doing to improve my relationships?

_____

_____

_____

_____

_____

5. One question for God today: write it on separate piece of paper, put in a prayer box and leave with it for him.

Sample Routine
(Self Employed)

6:00	Face/Prayer/Armor
6:30	Morning Cocktail & Bone broth
7:00	Breakfast/Bible Study
7:30	
8:00	Bounce & Breathe 10x
8:30	
9:00	Walk 15/Workout 15
9:30	Shower/Ready/ Affirmations
10:00	
10:30	Cleaning (see routine)
11:00	Write
11:30	
12:00	Lunch – Meeting?
12:30	Write
1:00	Emails/Calls/Apt
1:30	
2:00	
2:30	Bounce/Breathe 10min
3:00	Write
3:30	
4:00	Craft/Garden/Visit
4:30	
5:00	
5:30	
6:00	Make Dinner/Go Out
6:30	
7:00	Eat dinner/Watch T.V.
7:30	
8:00	Clean up Dinner
8:30	Walk 15min
9:00	Pamper
9:30	
10:00	Facial/Ready for Bed
10:30	Night Reflections
11:00	Bed

5:00 _____	4:30 _____
5:30 _____	5:00 _____
6:00 _____	5:30 _____
6:30 _____	6:00 _____
7:00 _____	6:30 _____
7:30 _____	7:00 _____
8:00 _____	7:30 _____
8:30 _____	8:00 _____
9:00 _____	8:30 _____
9:30 _____	9:00 _____
10:00 _____	9:30 _____
10:30 _____	10:00 _____
11:00 _____	10:30 _____
11:30 _____	11:00 _____
12:00 _____	11:30 _____
12:30 _____	12:00 _____
1:00 _____	12:30 _____
1:30 _____	1:00 _____
2:00 _____	1:30 _____
2:30 _____	2:00 _____
3:00 _____	2:30 _____
3:30 _____	3:00 _____
4:00 _____	

❦

APRIL

Birthdays

_____

_____

_____

_____

_____

_____

_____

_____

_____

PLANT TIPS

Dig up and separate perennial plants in Spring and Fall. Move where you like or give away. This prevents them getting rootbound and/or taking over.
Make sure to water newly planted plants.

Water outdoor potted plants, every day, unless they are cacti or succulents.

Be prepared to cover or move outdoor, potted plants out of the rain IF, they do not need watering.

Plants love company – the more you have the happier they will be. Imitate their habitat.

Cut back your remaining plant after it seeds. (starts appearing to die).

All homes have different atmospheres: lighting and air circulation. Move plants around to see what they like.

Start new plants with babies that emerge, to prevent **rootbound** plants. Cut or separate at root and place in water or dirt. Starts must have leaves to gather light and grow.

IF you LOVE plants in your home, but lack sunlight, try using plant lights in place of light bulbs. In low traffic areas.

- ACV & Dawn in saucer to prevent gnats.
- Ground eggshells to add calcium
- Dust your plant leaves with a soft brush
- Place plants on saucers/trays to add humidity to the air
- Cut brown tips off and follow the natural shape of leaf.

Repot plants when their pot looks full or like they need new/ more soil.

Make sure plants have drainage. Use stones in potting soil, sit on stone tray. This prevents **root rot.**

Prayer

Our Father in heaven, Hallowed be your name, Your kingdom come your will be done, on Earth as it is in Heaven. Give us today our Daily Bread and Forgive us our debts, as we also have forgiven our debtors. And lead us not into temptation but deliver us from the evil one. *Mathew 6:9-*

Christ-Like Qualities

Loving	Trusting
Courageous	Peaceful
Surrendered	Creative
Compassion	Honest
Mindful	Humble
Accepting	Bold
Considerate	Grateful
Dependable	Confident
Discerning	Curious
Compassion	Patient
Considerate	Kind
Productive	Forgiving
Obedience	Faithful
Perseverant	Discipline
Temperate	Integrity
Authenticity	Courteous
Generous	Respectful
Responsible	Patient
Unchanging	Wise
Righteous	Eternal
Omnipotent	Sovereign

Armor of God

Helmet of SALVATION -NOTHING can separate you from God. *Romans 8:38-39*

Breastplate of RIGHTOUSNESS - ALL your sins are covered; you are purified. *1 John 1:7*

Shield of FAITH - He works ALL things for our good. *Romans 8:28*

Belt of TRUTH - God's word breathes life into your soul. *Hebrews 4:12*

Sword of the SPIRIT, word of God. Speak it OUTLOUD, to defeat the enemy. *Mathew 17:20*

Shoes of PEACE – *Philippians 4:7* and the READINESS to SERVE. *Luke 12:43*

Affirmation

I am a

———————————————,

———————————————,

———————————————

child of God.

*Choose three qualities, from Christ-like Qualities List, you would like to become or improve on. Speak aloud every day. Change anytime.

Memory Verse

_____
_____
_____
_____
_____
_____
_____

Slow down....
Check your Choices & Responsibilities

Emotional IQ
Beliefs
Attitude
Intentions
Energy/Mood
Reactions/Responses
Actions/Behaviors
Decisions
Time

My Intention/Goal/Dream

_____
_____
_____
_____
_____
_____
_____
_____
_____

Morning Mindset

1. Who is one person I can lift up/help today?

_____
_____

How?

_____
_____

2. One action, I can take, to-ward MY Intention, Goal, Dream(s) today Is…

_____
_____
_____
_____

3. What is the cost if I do not take the action(s)?

_____
_____
_____
_____

4. What can I intentionally learn today to support myself?

_____
_____
_____
_____

5. What area of growth am I focusing on this week?

_____
_____
_____
_____

Anti-Aging Face Regimen

Morning
Wash face w/cleanser
Vitamin C Serum
Hyaluronic Acid
Sunscreen SPF15

Noon
Sunscreen SPF15
Hyaluronic Acid
Toner (see Recipe)

B4 Bed
Wash Face
Alpha Hydroxy Acid
Retinol
Hyaluronic Acid
*Try a moisturizer w/
hyaluronic acid.

Toner Recipe

Harvest/Purchase

a handful of

Cell Rejuvenating Herb

(Lavender or Rose)

Place into 12oz. boiling
spring water, and

Let it sit overnight.

Strain and put into

spray bottle.

Breathe & Meditate

Take 5 minutes to Step away from everyone and everything.

Sit quietly. Once you have settled. (Record yourself or someone, in a monotone voice, saying…)

Think of the most serene place, of which you can think. Breathe Deep. In through your nose. Out through your mouth.

In this place, what is the weather like? Think of how it smells.

Think of how it feels.

What do you see?

Imagine Jesus is there.

He walks toward you.

Can you take his hand?

If not, you can follow him. You begin walking together.

As you walk, just breathe.

Now, open your eyes.

*Do this every morning and anytime you need comfort, strength, peace.
** IF you are unable to take Jesus' hand, keep practicing and it will get easier.

3) Daily Gratitude's

_____

_____

_____

Whole Health Cocktail

(drink 4oz. Every Morning)

2T Apple Cider Vinegar
4T Lemon Juice
2c. Cranberry Juice
4c. Water
Follow w/8oz. Bone broth

Raise Your Energy

- Stand and Bounce on your toes every hour.
- Swing your arms in circles
- Take Deep Breaths 10x.
- Brisk 5-minute Walk
- Listen to Uplifting Music
- Take a cold shower
- Take Vitamin B12
- Drink Ginseng tea

Exercise Tips

- Eat protein after working out or strenuous activities.
- Drink water in ounces equal to half your body weight.
- Make sure your sleep is consistent. *Setting your internal clock enables your body in its healing process.
- While working out call an accountability partner.

Fitness Routine

Weight/Height = BMI

Yoga	_____min
Walk	_____min
Aerobics	_____min
Swim	_____min
Cycle	_____min
Hike	_____min

Strength Training

Reps/weight#

Shoulders	____/____
Arms	____/____
Abs	____/____
Chest	____/____
Legs	____/____
Buttocks	____/____
Core	____/____

*Max heart rate = 220 less Your Age **Low rate = Max multiplied by .65.

Arms – Shoulder pinches and rolls, push-ups, butterflies, Curl ups and Back Rows

Legs – Squats, Step ups, Ball squeezes, Kick backs

Core – Planks and Leg lifts

Cleaning Routine
(See check list in back of book)

Monday

_____
_____
_____

Tuesday

_____
_____
_____

Wednesday

_____
_____
_____

Thursday

_____
_____
_____

Friday

_____
_____
_____

Saturday

_____
_____
_____

Sunday

_____
_____
_____

MUST Do

_____
_____
_____
_____

NEED to Do

_____
_____
_____
_____

WANT to DO

_____
_____
_____
_____

Night Reflections

1. One thing I learned today.

_____

_____

_____

_____

2. What is one thing I can improve on/challenge myself.

_____

_____

_____

_____

_____

3. How am I eliminating distractions? Taking control of my time …

_____

_____

_____

_____

4. What am I doing to improve my relationships?

_____

_____

_____

_____

_____

5. One question for God today: write it on separate piece of paper, put in a prayer box and leave with it for him.

Sample Routine
(Self Employed)

6:00	Face/Prayer/Armor
6:30	Morning Cocktail & Bone broth
7:00	Breakfast/Bible Study
7:30	
8:00	Bounce & Breathe 10x
8:30	
9:00	Walk 15/Workout 15
9:30	Shower/Ready/ Affirmations
10:00	
10:30	Cleaning (see routine)
11:00	Write
11:30	
12:00	Lunch – Meeting?
12:30	Write
1:00	Emails/Calls/Apt
1:30	
2:00	
2:30	Bounce/Breathe 10min
3:00	Write
3:30	
4:00	Craft/Garden/Visit
4:30	
5:00	
5:30	
6:00	Make Dinner/Go Out
6:30	
7:00	Eat dinner/Watch T.V.
7:30	
8:00	Clean up Dinner
8:30	Walk 15min
9:00	Pamper
9:30	
10:00	Facial/Ready for Bed
10:30	Night Reflections
11:00	Bed

5:00 _____

5:30 _____

6:00 _____

6:30 _____

7:00 _____

7:30 _____

8:00 _____

8:30 _____

9:00 _____

9:30 _____

10:00 _____

10:30 _____

11:00 _____

11:30 _____

12:00 _____

12:30 _____

1:00 _____

1:30 _____

2:00 _____

2:30 _____

3:00 _____

3:30 _____

4:00 _____

4:30 _____

5:00 _____

5:30 _____

6:00 _____

6:30 _____

7:00 _____

7:30 _____

8:00 _____

8:30 _____

9:00 _____

9:30 _____

10:00 _____

10:30 _____

11:00 _____

11:30 _____

12:00 _____

12:30 _____

1:00 _____

1:30 _____

2:00 _____

2:30 _____

3:00 _____

MAY

Birthdays

_____

_____

_____

_____

_____

_____

_____

_____

GET OUT OF DEBT & SAVE!

1. Freeze Your Spending

2. 70% Living & 30% Tithe, Save, and Spend

*Starting out, you may have to use your 30% until you get your living expenses down to 70%.

3. Break down ALL expenses into weekly bills.

4. Subtract ALL expense amount from 70% of income. Use remaining to extra and Pay Off one debt at a time.

5. Create a 'Motivational' list of all outside debts, from lowest amount to largest, and mark out as you pay off.

6. Roll over money from Paid Off expense to next debt.

7. After paying off debt, build your credit:

- $500 secured loans.
- Obtain a secured credit card.
- Utilize CD's
- Cash back cards
- Round Up program(s)

Possible Expenses

Tithing/Charities
Phone
Auto Payment
Auto Insurance
Gas
Mortgage/Rent
Electric
Heat
Water
Groceries
Hygiene
Trash
Child Support
Baby Sitting
Pets
School Supplies
Clothing
Health Insurance
Credit Card Debt
School Loans
Personal Loans
Medical
Media
Entertainment
Birthdays
Holidays
Vacations
Subscription Dues
Membership Fees
Dining Out
House Cleaning

Prayer

Our Father in heaven, Hallowed
be your name, Your kingdom
come your will be done, on Earth
as it is in Heaven. Give us today
our Daily Bread and Forgive
us our debts, as we also have
forgiven our debtors. And lead us
not into temptation but deliver us
from the evil one. *Mathew 6:9-*

Christ-Like Qualities

Loving	Trusting
Courageous	Peaceful
Surrendered	Creative
Compassion	Honest
Mindful	Humble
Accepting	Bold
Considerate	Grateful
Dependable	Confident
Discerning	Curious
Compassion	Patient
Considerate	Kind
Productive	Forgiving
Obedience	Faithful
Perseverant	Discipline
Temperate	Integrity
Authenticity	Courteous
Generous	Respectful
Responsible	Patient
Unchanging	Wise
Righteous	Eternal
Omnipotent	Sovereign

Armor of God

Helmet of
SALVATION -NOTHING can
separate you from God.
Romans 8:38-39

Breastplate of
RIGHTOUSNESS - ALL your
sins are covered; you are purified.
1 John 1:7

Shield of FAITH - He works ALL
things for our good. *Romans 8:28*

Belt of TRUTH - God's word
breathes life into your soul.
Hebrews 4:12

Sword of the SPIRIT, word of
God. Speak it OUTLOUD, to
defeat the enemy. *Mathew 17:20*

Shoes of PEACE – *Philippians 4:7*
and the READINESS to SERVE.
Luke 12:43

Affirmation

I am a

_____,

_____,

_____
child of God.
*Choose three qualities, from Christ-like
Qualities List, you would like to become
or improve on. Speak aloud every day.
Change anytime.

Memory Verse

_____
_____
_____
_____
_____
_____
_____

Slow down....
Check your Choices & Responsibilities

Emotional IQ
Beliefs
Attitude
Intentions
Energy/Mood
Reactions/Responses
Actions/Behaviors
Decisions
Time

My Intention/Goal/Dream

_____
_____
_____
_____
_____
_____
_____
_____
_____

Morning Mindset

1. Who is one person I can lift up/help today?

_____
_____

How?

_____
_____

2. One action, I can take, to-ward MY Intention, Goal, Dream(s) today Is…

_____
_____
_____
_____

3. What is the cost if I do not take the action(s)?

_____
_____
_____
_____

4. What can I intentionally learn today to support myself?

_____
_____
_____

5. What area of growth am I focusing on this week?

_____
_____
_____

Anti-Aging Face Regimen

Morning
Wash face w/cleanser
Vitamin C Serum
Hyaluronic Acid
Sunscreen SPF15

Noon
Sunscreen SPF15
Hyaluronic Acid
Toner (see Recipe)

B4 Bed
Wash Face
Alpha Hydroxy Acid
Retinol
Hyaluronic Acid
*Try a moisturizer w/
hyaluronic acid.

Toner Recipe

Harvest/Purchase

a handful of

Cell Rejuvenating Herb

(Lavender or Rose)

Place into 12oz. boiling
spring water, and

Let it sit overnight.

Strain and put into

spray bottle.

Breathe & Meditate

Take 5 minutes to Step away from everyone and everything.

Sit quietly. Once you have settled. (Record yourself or someone, in a monotone voice, saying…)

Think of the most serene place, of which you can think. Breathe Deep. In through your nose. Out through your mouth.

In this place, what is the weather like? Think of how it smells.

Think of how it feels.

What do you see?

Imagine Jesus is there.

He walks toward you.

Can you take his hand?

If not, you can follow him. You begin walking together.

As you walk, just breathe.

Now, open your eyes.

*Do this every morning and anytime you need comfort, strength, peace. ** IF you are unable to take Jesus' hand, keep practicing and it will get easier.

3) Daily Gratitude's

_____

_____

_____

Whole Health Cocktail
(drink 4oz. Every Morning)

2T Apple Cider Vinegar
4T Lemon Juice
2c. Cranberry Juice
4c. Water
Follow w/8oz. Bone broth

Raise Your Energy

- Stand and Bounce on your toes every hour.
- Swing your arms in circles
- Take Deep Breaths 10x.
- Brisk 5-minute Walk
- Listen to Uplifting Music
- Take a cold shower
- Take Vitamin B12
- Drink Ginseng tea

Exercise Tips

- Eat protein after working out or strenuous activities.
- Drink water in ounces equal to half your body weight.
- Make sure your sleep is consistent. *Setting your internal clock enables your body in its healing process.
- While working out call an accountability partner.

Fitness Routine
Weight/Height = BMI

Yoga	_____min
Walk	_____min
Aerobics	_____min
Swim	_____min
Cycle	_____min
Hike	_____min

Strength Training
Reps/weight#

Shoulders	___/___
Arms	___/___
Abs	___/___
Chest	___/___
Legs	___/___
Buttocks	___/___
Core	___/___

*Max heart rate = 220 less Your Age **Low rate = Max multiplied by .65.

Arms – Shoulder pinches and rolls, push-ups, butterflies, Curl ups and Back Rows

Legs – Squats, Step ups, Ball squeezes, Kick backs

Core – Planks and Leg lifts

__Cleaning Routine__
(See check list in back of book)

Monday
_____
_____
_____

Tuesday
_____
_____
_____

Wednesday
_____
_____
_____

Thursday
_____
_____
_____

Friday
_____
_____
_____

Saturday
_____
_____
_____

Sunday
_____
_____
_____

MUST Do
_____
_____
_____

NEED to Do
_____
_____
_____

WANT to DO
_____
_____
_____

Night Reflections

1. One thing I learned today.

_____
_____
_____
_____

2. What is one thing I can improve on/challenge myself.

_____
_____
_____
_____
_____

3. How am I eliminating distractions? Taking control of my time …

_____
_____
_____
_____

4. What am I doing to improve my relationships?

_____
_____
_____
_____
_____

5. One question for God today: write it on separate piece of paper, put in a prayer box and leave with it for him.

Sample Routine
(Self Employed)

6:00	Face/Prayer/Armor
6:30	Morning Cocktail & Bone broth
7:00	Breakfast/Bible Study
7:30	
8:00	Bounce & Breathe 10x
8:30	
9:00	Walk 15/Workout 15
9:30	Shower/Ready/Affirmations
10:00	
10:30	Cleaning (see routine)
11:00	Write
11:30	
12:00	Lunch – Meeting?
12:30	Write
1:00	Emails/Calls/Apt
1:30	
2:00	
2:30	Bounce/Breathe 10min
3:00	Write
3:30	
4:00	Craft/Garden/Visit
4:30	
5:00	
5:30	
6:00	Make Dinner/Go Out
6:30	
7:00	Eat dinner/Watch T.V.
7:30	
8:00	Clean up Dinner
8:30	Walk 15min
9:00	Pamper
9:30	
10:00	Facial/Ready for Bed
10:30	Night Reflections
11:00	Bed

5:00 _____	4:30 _____
5:30 _____	5:00 _____
6:00 _____	5:30 _____
6:30 _____	6:00 _____
7:00 _____	6:30 _____
7:30 _____	7:00 _____
8:00 _____	7:30 _____
8:30 _____	8:00 _____
9:00 _____	8:30 _____
9:30 _____	9:00 _____
10:00 _____	9:30 _____
10:30 _____	10:00 _____
11:00 _____	10:30 _____
11:30 _____	11:00 _____
12:00 _____	11:30 _____
12:30 _____	12:00 _____
1:00 _____	12:30 _____
1:30 _____	1:00 _____
2:00 _____	1:30 _____
2:30 _____	2:00 _____
3:00 _____	2:30 _____
3:30 _____	3:00 _____
4:00 _____	

JUNE

Birthdays

_____

_____

_____

_____

_____

_____

_____

_____

_____

GAINING MENTAL CLARITY

What you think becomes your belief and determines YOUR **Perspective** (the lens), which you filter ALL of your experiences, as you go into the world. *For as he thinketh in his heart, so is he. Proverbs 23:7*

We demolish arguments and every pretension that sets itself up against the knowledge of God, and we take captive every thought to make it obedient to Christ. 2 Corinthians 10:5

Is your mental health/thought life keeping you in Spiritual Bondage? The following questions will assist you in uncovering your thought and belief patterns.

People cannot teach what they have not been taught; what they do not know. *For all have sinned and fall short of the glory of God, Romans 3:23*

When you were a child:
Were there any Expectations? Were they age appropriate/realistic? What were you expected to do? How were you expected to behave? Was perfection an expectation? What expectations do you have for yourself today? Do they resemble childhood expectations? What are you expecting from others? i.e., Mom, Dad, siblings, children, boss, friends, etc....

Criticism and **Perfectionism** are forms of **Judgement**, which can cause people to think and believe they are 'not good enough.' *Do not let any unwholesome talk come out of your mouths, but only what is helpful for building others up according to their needs, that it may benefit those who listen. Ephesians 4:29*

Is your Spiritual belief system grounded in what the world says or what God says? Here are affirmation verses, to help you think about who you are in Christ, verses what the world has led you to believe. If you believe God's word was written for you. He says...

Were you criticized? For what? Can you see this in your life today? Are you critical of others? Hard on yourself? Were you judged? How? For what? i.e., behaviors, personality, characteristics, etc. Can you see how you may be judging others?

I am Forgiven	I have a Powerful Loving Mind	I am Gods Temple
I am Predestined	I am Co-heir with Christ	I am a Child of God
I am Chosen	I am a Masterpiece	I am Made New

Awareness enables you to **overcome strongholds, by choosing your beliefs**, about yourself, others, the world around you, and what best serves you in your relationship with God.

Don't you know that you, yourselves are God's temple and that God's Spirit dwells in your midst? *1 Corinthians 3:16*	For the Spirit God gave us does not make us timid; but gives us power, love, and self- discipline. *2 Timothy 1:7*	Therefore, there is now, no condemnation, for those who are in Christ Jesus. *Romans 8:1*
So you are no longer a slave, but God's child; and since you are his child, God has made you also an heir. *Galatians 4:7*	Now if we are children, then heirs - heirs of God and co-heirs with Christ, if indeed we share in his sufferings in order that we may also share in his glory. *Romans 8:17*	For those he foreknew he also predestined to be conformed to the image of his Son, that he might be the firstborn among many brothers and sisters. *Romans 8:29*
Therefore, if anyone is in Christ, the new creation has come; The old has gone, the new is here! *2 Corinthians 5:17*	For we are God's handiwork, created in Christ Jesus to do good works, which God prepared in advance for us to do. *Ephesians 2:10*	You did not choose me, but I chose you and appointed you so that you might go and bear fruit – fruit that will last... *John 15:16*

Prayer

Our Father in heaven, Hallowed
be your name, Your kingdom
come your will be done, on Earth
as it is in Heaven. Give us today
our Daily Bread and Forgive
us our debts, as we also have
forgiven our debtors. And lead us
not into temptation but deliver us
from the evil one. *Mathew 6:9-*

Christ-Like Qualities

Loving	Trusting
Courageous	Peaceful
Surrendered	Creative
Compassion	Honest
Mindful	Humble
Accepting	Bold
Considerate	Grateful
Dependable	Confident
Discerning	Curious
Compassion	Patient
Considerate	Kind
Productive	Forgiving
Obedience	Faithful
Perseverant	Discipline
Temperate	Integrity
Authenticity	Courteous
Generous	Respectful
Responsible	Patient
Unchanging	Wise
Righteous	Eternal
Omnipotent	Sovereign

Armor of God

Helmet of
SALVATION -NOTHING can
separate you from God.
Romans 8:38-39

Breastplate of
RIGHTOUSNESS - ALL your
sins are covered; you are purified.
1 John 1:7

Shield of FAITH - He works ALL
things for our good. *Romans 8:28*

Belt of TRUTH - God's word
breathes life into your soul.
Hebrews 4:12

Sword of the SPIRIT, word of
God. Speak it OUTLOUD, to
defeat the enemy. *Mathew 17:20*

Shoes of PEACE – *Philippians 4:7*
and the READINESS to SERVE.
Luke 12:43

Affirmation

I am a

_____,
_____,
_____
child of God.
*Choose three qualities, from Christ-like
Qualities List, you would like to become
or improve on. Speak aloud every day.
Change anytime.

Memory Verse

_____
_____
_____
_____
_____
_____
_____

Slow down....
Check your Choices & Responsibilities

Emotional IQ
Beliefs
Attitude
Intentions
Energy/Mood
Reactions/Responses
Actions/Behaviors
Decisions
Time

My Intention/Goal/Dream

_____
_____
_____
_____
_____
_____
_____
_____
_____

Morning Mindset

1. Who is one person I can lift up/help today?

_____
_____

How?

_____
_____

2. One action, I can take, to-ward MY Intention, Goal, Dream(s) today Is…

_____
_____
_____
_____

3. What is the cost if I do not take the action(s)?

_____
_____
_____
_____

4. What can I intentionally learn today to support myself?

_____
_____
_____

5. What area of growth am I focusing on this week?

_____
_____
_____

Anti-Aging Face Regimen

Morning
Wash face w/cleanser
Vitamin C Serum
Hyaluronic Acid
Sunscreen SPF15

Noon
Sunscreen SPF15
Hyaluronic Acid
Toner (see Recipe)

B4 Bed
Wash Face
Alpha Hydroxy Acid
Retinol
Hyaluronic Acid
*Try a moisturizer w/
hyaluronic acid.

Toner Recipe

Harvest/Purchase

a handful of

Cell Rejuvenating Herb

(Lavender or Rose)

Place into 12oz. boiling
spring water, and

Let it sit overnight.

Strain and put into

spray bottle.

Breathe & Meditate

Take 5 minutes to Step away from everyone and everything.

Sit quietly. Once you have settled. (Record yourself or someone, in a monotone voice, saying…)

Think of the most serene place, of which you can think. Breathe Deep. In through your nose. Out through your mouth.

In this place, what is the weather like? Think of how it smells.

Think of how it feels.

What do you see?

Imagine Jesus is there.

He walks toward you.

Can you take his hand?

If not, you can follow him. You begin walking together.

As you walk, just breathe.

Now, open your eyes.

*Do this every morning and anytime you need comfort, strength, peace.
** IF you are unable to take Jesus' hand, keep practicing and it will get easier.

3) Daily Gratitude's

_____

_____

_____

Whole Health Cocktail
(drink 4oz. Every Morning)

2T Apple Cider Vinegar
4T Lemon Juice
2c. Cranberry Juice
4c. Water
Follow w/8oz. Bone broth

Raise Your Energy

- Stand and Bounce on your toes every hour.
- Swing your arms in circles
- Take Deep Breaths 10x.
- Brisk 5-minute Walk
- Listen to Uplifting Music
- Take a cold shower
- Take Vitamin B12
- Drink Ginseng tea

Exercise Tips

- Eat protein after working out or strenuous activities.
- Drink water in ounces equal to half your body weight.
- Make sure your sleep is consistent. *Setting your internal clock enables your body in its healing process.
- While working out call an accountability partner.

Fitness Routine
Weight/Height = BMI

Yoga	____min
Walk	____min
Aerobics	____min
Swim	____min
Cycle	____min
Hike	____min

Strength Training
Reps/weight#

Shoulders	___/___
Arms	___/___
Abs	___/___
Chest	___/___
Legs	___/___
Buttocks	___/___
Core	___/___

*Max heart rate = 220 less Your Age **Low rate = Max multiplied by .65.

Arms – Shoulder pinches and rolls, push-ups, butterflies, Curl ups and Back Rows

Legs – Squats, Step ups, Ball squeezes, Kick backs

Core – Planks and Leg lifts

Cleaning Routine
(See check list in back of book)

Monday

_____
_____
_____

Tuesday

_____
_____
_____

Wednesday

_____
_____
_____

Thursday

_____
_____
_____

Friday

_____
_____
_____

Saturday

_____
_____
_____

Sunday

_____
_____
_____

MUST Do

_____
_____
_____
_____

NEED to Do

_____
_____
_____
_____

WANT to DO

_____
_____
_____
_____

Night Reflections

1. One thing I learned today.

_____

_____

_____

_____

2. What is one thing I can improve on/challenge myself.

_____

_____

_____

_____

_____

3. How am I eliminating distractions? Taking control of my time …

_____

_____

_____

_____

4. What am I doing to improve my relationships?

_____

_____

_____

_____

_____

5. One question for God today: write it on separate piece of paper, put in a prayer box and leave with it for him.

Sample Routine
(Self Employed)

6:00	_Face/Prayer/Armor_
6:30	_Morning Cocktail &_
	Bone broth
7:00	_Breakfast/Bible Study_
7:30	
8:00	_Bounce & Breathe 10x_
8:30	
9:00	_Walk 15/Workout 15_
9:30	_Shower/Ready/_
	Affirmations
10:00	
10:30	_Cleaning (see routine)_
11:00	_Write_
11:30	
12:00	_Lunch – Meeting?_
12:30	_Write_
1:00	_Emails/Calls/Apt_
1:30	
2:00	
2:30	_Bounce/Breathe 10min_
3:00	_Write_
3:30	
4:00	_Craft/Garden/Visit_
4:30	
5:00	
5:30	
6:00	_Make Dinner/Go Out_
6:30	
7:00	_Eat dinner/Watch T.V._
7:30	
8:00	_Clean up Dinner_
8:30	_Walk 15min_
9:00	_Pamper_
9:30	
10:00	_Facial/Ready for Bed_
10:30	_Night Reflections_
11:00	_Bed_

5:00 _____

5:30 _____

6:00 _____

6:30 _____

7:00 _____

7:30 _____

8:00 _____

8:30 _____

9:00 _____

9:30 _____

10:00 _____

10:30 _____

11:00 _____

11:30 _____

12:00 _____

12:30 _____

1:00 _____

1:30 _____

2:00 _____

2:30 _____

3:00 _____

3:30 _____

4:00 _____

4:30 _____

5:00 _____

5:30 _____

6:00 _____

6:30 _____

7:00 _____

7:30 _____

8:00 _____

8:30 _____

9:00 _____

9:30 _____

10:00 _____

10:30 _____

11:00 _____

11:30 _____

12:00 _____

12:30 _____

1:00 _____

1:30 _____

2:00 _____

2:30 _____

3:00 _____

JULY

Birthdays

_____

_____

_____

_____

_____

_____

_____

_____

_____

SPIRITUAL ROOTS

Now that you have background, on your past life, you can grow in your identity in Christ, by uprooting the enemies lies and replacing them with God's truth. *Do not conform to the pattern of this world but be transformed by the renewing of your mind. Then you will be able to test and approve what God's will is... Romans 12:2*

The enemy has one agenda: to lie, steal and destroy; your relationships, finances, health, mind, emotions, etc....

Be alert and of sober mind. Your enemy the devil prowls around like a roaring lion looking for someone to devour.
1 Peter 5:8

> **Time** – What type of Distractions are hindering your walk with Jesus today? Are they reminiscent of your youth? (i.e., Money, Possessions, Relationships, Entertainment, Addictions, etc.)

The enemy schemes to keep us quiet through fear: intimidation, acts of violence, ridicule, ignorance, etc. However, the Lord says we are to verbally rebuke the enemy, we are to confront others, we are to spread his word, and be bold about it - NOT BE QUIET! Please read: *Mathew 18:15-17* and *Mathew 7:1-5*

Whoever hates reproof will die. Proverbs 15:10 Better is open rebuke, than hidden love. Proverbs 27:5

> **Communication** – How have you been exposed to fear? Have you spoken about it? How has it affected your life choices? Do you speak your truth; what you want, do not want, like and do not like, your goals and dreams; needs and desires, etc....? Have you confronted others with love? Have you forgiven them? Have you asked forgiveness?

Prayer

Our Father in heaven, Hallowed be your name, Your kingdom come your will be done, on Earth as it is in Heaven. Give us today our Daily Bread and Forgive us our debts, as we also have forgiven our debtors. And lead us not into temptation but deliver us from the evil one. *Mathew 6:9-*

Christ-Like Qualities

Loving	Trusting
Courageous	Peaceful
Surrendered	Creative
Compassion	Honest
Mindful	Humble
Accepting	Bold
Considerate	Grateful
Dependable	Confident
Discerning	Curious
Compassion	Patient
Considerate	Kind
Productive	Forgiving
Obedience	Faithful
Perseverant	Discipline
Temperate	Integrity
Authenticity	Courteous
Generous	Respectful
Responsible	Patient
Unchanging	Wise
Righteous	Eternal
Omnipotent	Sovereign

Armor of God

Helmet of SALVATION -NOTHING can separate you from God. *Romans 8:38-39*

Breastplate of RIGHTOUSNESS - ALL your sins are covered; you are purified. *1 John 1:7*

Shield of FAITH - He works ALL things for our good. *Romans 8:28*

Belt of TRUTH - God's word breathes life into your soul. *Hebrews 4:12*

Sword of the SPIRIT, word of God. Speak it OUTLOUD, to defeat the enemy. *Mathew 17:20*

Shoes of PEACE – *Philippians 4:7* and the READINESS to SERVE. *Luke 12:43*

Affirmation

I am a

_____,

_____,

_____

child of God.

*Choose three qualities, from Christ-like Qualities List, you would like to become or improve on. Speak aloud every day. Change anytime.

Memory Verse

_____
_____
_____
_____
_____
_____
_____

Slow down....
Check your Choices & Responsibilities

Emotional IQ
Beliefs
Attitude
Intentions
Energy/Mood
Reactions/Responses
Actions/Behaviors
Decisions
Time

My Intention/Goal/Dream

_____
_____
_____
_____
_____
_____
_____
_____
_____
_____
_____

Morning Mindset

1. Who is one person I can lift up/help today?

_____
_____

How?

_____
_____

2. One action, I can take, to-ward MY Intention, Goal, Dream(s) today Is...

_____
_____
_____
_____

3. What is the cost if I do not take the action(s)?

_____
_____
_____
_____

4. What can I intentionally learn today to support myself?

_____
_____
_____

5. What area of growth am I focusing on this week?

_____
_____
_____

Anti-Aging Face Regimen

Morning
Wash face w/cleanser
Vitamin C Serum
Hyaluronic Acid
Sunscreen SPF15

Noon
Sunscreen SPF15
Hyaluronic Acid
Toner (see Recipe)

B4 Bed
Wash Face
Alpha Hydroxy Acid
Retinol
Hyaluronic Acid
*Try a moisturizer w/
hyaluronic acid.

Toner Recipe

Harvest/Purchase

a handful of

Cell Rejuvenating Herb

(Lavender or Rose)

Place into 12oz. boiling
spring water, and

Let it sit overnight.

Strain and put into

spray bottle.

Breathe & Meditate

Take 5 minutes to Step away from everyone and everything.

Sit quietly. Once you have settled. (Record yourself or someone, in a monotone voice, saying...)

Think of the most serene place, of which you can think. Breathe Deep. In through your nose. Out through your mouth.

In this place, what is the weather like? Think of how it smells.

Think of how it feels.

What do you see?

Imagine Jesus is there.

He walks toward you.

Can you take his hand?

If not, you can follow him. You begin walking together.

As you walk, just breathe.

Now, open your eyes.

*Do this every morning and anytime you need comfort, strength, peace.
** IF you are unable to take Jesus' hand, keep practicing and it will get easier.

3) Daily Gratitude's

_____

_____

_____

Whole Health Cocktail

(drink 4oz. Every Morning)

2T Apple Cider Vinegar
4T Lemon Juice
2c. Cranberry Juice
4c. Water
Follow w/8oz. Bone broth

Raise Your Energy

* Stand and Bounce on your toes every hour.
* Swing your arms in circles
* Take Deep Breaths 10x.
* Brisk 5-minute Walk
* Listen to Uplifting Music
* Take a cold shower
* Take Vitamin B12
* Drink Ginseng tea

Exercise Tips

* Eat protein after working out or strenuous activities.
* Drink water in ounces equal to half your body weight.
* Make sure your sleep is consistent. *Setting your internal clock enables your body in its healing process.
* While working out call an accountability partner.

Fitness Routine

Weight/Height = BMI

Yoga	_____min
Walk	_____min
Aerobics	_____min
Swim	_____min
Cycle	_____min
Hike	_____min

Strength Training

Reps/weight#

Shoulders	____/____
Arms	____/____
Abs	____/____
Chest	____/____
Legs	____/____
Buttocks	____/____
Core	____/____

*Max heart rate = 220 less Your Age **Low rate = Max multiplied by .65.

Arms – Shoulder pinches and rolls, push-ups, butterflies, Curl ups and Back Rows

Legs – Squats, Step ups, Ball squeezes, Kick backs

Core – Planks and Leg lifts

Cleaning Routine
(See check list in back of book)

Monday
_____
_____
_____

Tuesday
_____
_____
_____

Wednesday
_____
_____
_____

Thursday
_____
_____
_____

Friday
_____
_____
_____

Saturday
_____
_____
_____

Sunday
_____
_____
_____

MUST Do
_____
_____
_____

NEED to Do
_____
_____
_____

WANT to DO
_____
_____
_____

Night Reflections

Sample Routine
(Self Employed)

1. One thing I learned today.

_____
_____
_____
_____

2. What is one thing I can improve on/challenge myself.

_____
_____
_____
_____
_____

3. How am I eliminating distractions? Taking control of my time …

_____
_____
_____
_____

4. What am I doing to improve my relationships?

_____
_____
_____
_____
_____

5. One question for God today: write it on separate piece of paper, put in a prayer box and leave with it for him.

6:00	Face/Prayer/Armor
6:30	Morning Cocktail & Bone broth
7:00	Breakfast/Bible Study
7:30	
8:00	Bounce & Breathe 10x
8:30	
9:00	Walk 15/Workout 15
9:30	Shower/Ready/ Affirmations
10:00	
10:30	Cleaning (see routine)
11:00	Write
11:30	
12:00	Lunch – Meeting?
12:30	Write
1:00	Emails/Calls/Apt
1:30	
2:00	
2:30	Bounce/Breathe 10min
3:00	Write
3:30	
4:00	Craft/Garden/Visit
4:30	
5:00	
5:30	
6:00	Make Dinner/Go Out
6:30	
7:00	Eat dinner/Watch T.V.
7:30	
8:00	Clean up Dinner
8:30	Walk 15min
9:00	Pamper
9:30	
10:00	Facial/Ready for Bed
10:30	Night Reflections
11:00	Bed

5:00 _____

5:30 _____

6:00 _____

6:30 _____

7:00 _____

7:30 _____

8:00 _____

8:30 _____

9:00 _____

9:30 _____

10:00 _____

10:30 _____

11:00 _____

11:30 _____

12:00 _____

12:30 _____

1:00 _____

1:30 _____

2:00 _____

2:30 _____

3:00 _____

3:30 _____

4:00 _____

4:30 _____

5:00 _____

5:30 _____

6:00 _____

6:30 _____

7:00 _____

7:30 _____

8:00 _____

8:30 _____

9:00 _____

9:30 _____

10:00 _____

10:30 _____

11:00 _____

11:30 _____

12:00 _____

12:30 _____

1:00 _____

1:30 _____

2:00 _____

2:30 _____

3:00 _____

AUGUST

Birthdays

_____

_____

_____

_____

_____

_____

_____

_____

EMOTIONAL IQ

Now that you are aware of your 'worldly' view, verses that of Christ, can you see how your thoughts and beliefs can affect your emotions? i.e., Negativity, anger, jealousy, distrust, low self-esteem, fear, anxiety, stress, depression, etc....

The Lord says to come to him broken and he will restore what was stolen. *After you have suffered a little while, the God of grace, who has called you to his eternal glory in Christ, will himself restore, confirm, strengthen, and establish you.1 Peter 5:10*

> What emotions/feelings come up when you think about your childhood experiences and relationships, adult experiences, past relationships, religious experiences, etc.

We can be stuck in our emotions because they are tied to unresolved issues. Issues left unresolved because we lacked the cognitive ability to understand, communication and coping skills to resolve things.

Instead, we learned to turn our emotions inward, using defense mechanisms; **repression** or **minimizing** the experience, **denial** of it ever happening or **projecting** our experience, as though it happened to someone else, **blaming** others, becoming **defensive**, etc. – never receiving validation. Validation is needed for resolution.

Learning to resolve issues is needed to get past the hurt, pain, betrayal, loss, etc. and how we rise to our full potential and self-actualize. However, unmet needs of love and acceptance, security and stability, validation and approval, boundaries, coping skills, etc. hinder our emotional IQ; causing us to remain in our childish ways – seeking to fulfill unmet needs.

> Do you have any unresolved issues? Can you recognize defense mechanisms you have been using? Any unfulfilled needs? How was love shown? How were you disciplined? Could you talk about your feelings? Did you feel safe? Could you be your own person?

Prayer

Our Father in heaven, Hallowed be your name, Your kingdom come your will be done, on Earth as it is in Heaven. Give us today our Daily Bread and Forgive us our debts, as we also have forgiven our debtors. And lead us not into temptation but deliver us from the evil one. *Mathew 6:9-*

Christ-Like Qualities

Loving	Trusting
Courageous	Peaceful
Surrendered	Creative
Compassion	Honest
Mindful	Humble
Accepting	Bold
Considerate	Grateful
Dependable	Confident
Discerning	Curious
Compassion	Patient
Considerate	Kind
Productive	Forgiving
Obedience	Faithful
Perseverant	Discipline
Temperate	Integrity
Authenticity	Courteous
Generous	Respectful
Responsible	Patient
Unchanging	Wise
Righteous	Eternal
Omnipotent	Sovereign

Armor of God

Helmet of SALVATION -NOTHING can separate you from God. *Romans 8:38-39*

Breastplate of RIGHTOUSNESS - ALL your sins are covered; you are purified. *1 John 1:7*

Shield of FAITH - He works ALL things for our good. *Romans 8:28*

Belt of TRUTH - God's word breathes life into your soul. *Hebrews 4:12*

Sword of the SPIRIT, word of God. Speak it OUTLOUD, to defeat the enemy. *Mathew 17:20*

Shoes of PEACE – *Philippians 4:7* and the READINESS to SERVE. *Luke 12:43*

Affirmation

I am a

_____,

_____,

_____

child of God.

*Choose three qualities, from Christ-like Qualities List, you would like to become or improve on. Speak aloud every day. Change anytime.

Memory Verse

_____

_____

_____

_____

_____

_____

_____

Slow down....
Check your Choices &
Responsibilities

Emotional IQ

Beliefs

Attitude

Intentions

Energy/Mood

Reactions/Responses

Actions/Behaviors

Decisions

Time

My Intention/Goal/Dream

_____

_____

_____

_____

_____

_____

_____

_____

_____

Morning Mindset

1. Who is one person I can lift up/help today?

_____

_____

How?

_____

_____

2. One action, I can take, to-ward MY Intention, Goal, Dream(s) today Is…

_____

_____

_____

_____

3. What is the cost if I do not take the action(s)?

_____

_____

_____

_____

4. What can I intentionally learn today to support myself?

_____

_____

_____

_____

5. What area of growth am I focusing on this week?

_____

_____

Anti-Aging Face Regimen

Morning
Wash face w/cleanser
Vitamin C Serum
Hyaluronic Acid
Sunscreen SPF15

Noon
Sunscreen SPF15
Hyaluronic Acid
Toner (see Recipe)

B4 Bed
Wash Face
Alpha Hydroxy Acid
Retinol
Hyaluronic Acid
*Try a moisturizer w/
hyaluronic acid.

Toner Recipe

Harvest/Purchase
a handful of
Cell Rejuvenating Herb
(Lavender or Rose)
Place into 12oz. boiling
spring water, and
Let it sit overnight.
Strain and put into
spray bottle.

Breathe & Meditate

Take 5 minutes to Step away from everyone and everything.

Sit quietly. Once you have settled. (Record yourself or someone, in a monotone voice, saying...)

Think of the most serene place, of which you can think. Breathe Deep. In through your nose. Out through your mouth.

In this place, what is the weather like? Think of how it smells.

Think of how it feels.

What do you see?

Imagine Jesus is there.

He walks toward you.

Can you take his hand?

If not, you can follow him. You begin walking together.

As you walk, just breathe.

Now, open your eyes.

*Do this every morning and anytime you need comfort, strength, peace.
** IF you are unable to take Jesus' hand, keep practicing and it will get easier.

3) Daily Gratitude's

_____

_____

_____

Whole Health Cocktail
(drink 4oz. Every Morning)

2T Apple Cider Vinegar
4T Lemon Juice
2c. Cranberry Juice
4c. Water
Follow w/8oz. Bone broth

Raise Your Energy

- Stand and Bounce on your toes every hour.
- Swing your arms in circles
- Take Deep Breaths 10x.
- Brisk 5-minute Walk
- Listen to Uplifting Music
- Take a cold shower
- Take Vitamin B12
- Drink Ginseng tea

Exercise Tips

- Eat protein after working out or strenuous activities.
- Drink water in ounces equal to half your body weight.
- Make sure your sleep is consistent. *Setting your internal clock enables your body in its healing process.
- While working out call an accountability partner.

Fitness Routine
Weight/Height = BMI

Yoga	____min
Walk	____min
Aerobics	____min
Swim	____min
Cycle	____min
Hike	____min

Strength Training
Reps/weight#

Shoulders	____/____
Arms	____/____
Abs	____/____
Chest	____/____
Legs	____/____
Buttocks	____/____
Core	____/____

*Max heart rate = 220 less Your Age **Low rate = Max multiplied by .65.

Arms – Shoulder pinches and rolls, push-ups, butterflies, Curl ups and Back Rows

Legs – Squats, Step ups, Ball squeezes, Kick backs

Core – Planks and Leg lifts

Cleaning Routine
(See check list in back of book)

Monday

_____
_____
_____

Tuesday

_____
_____
_____

Wednesday

_____
_____
_____

Thursday

_____
_____
_____

Friday

_____
_____
_____

Saturday

_____
_____
_____

Sunday

_____
_____
_____

MUST Do

_____

_____

_____

NEED to Do

_____

_____

_____

_____

WANT to DO

_____

_____

_____

Night Reflections

1. One thing I learned today.

_____
_____
_____
_____

2. What is one thing I can improve on/challenge myself.

_____
_____
_____
_____

3. How am I eliminating distractions? Taking control of my time …

_____
_____
_____
_____

4. What am I doing to improve my relationships?

_____
_____
_____
_____

5. One question for God today: write it on separate piece of paper, put in a prayer box and leave with it for him.

Sample Routine
(Self Employed)

6:00	Face/Prayer/Armor
6:30	Morning Cocktail & Bone broth
7:00	Breakfast/Bible Study
7:30	
8:00	Bounce & Breathe 10x
8:30	
9:00	Walk 15/Workout 15
9:30	Shower/Ready/Affirmations
10:00	
10:30	Cleaning (see routine)
11:00	Write
11:30	
12:00	Lunch – Meeting?
12:30	Write
1:00	Emails/Calls/Apt
1:30	
2:00	
2:30	Bounce/Breathe 10min
3:00	Write
3:30	
4:00	Craft/Garden/Visit
4:30	
5:00	
5:30	
6:00	Make Dinner/Go Out
6:30	
7:00	Eat dinner/Watch T.V.
7:30	
8:00	Clean up Dinner
8:30	Walk 15min
9:00	Pamper
9:30	
10:00	Facial/Ready for Bed
10:30	Night Reflections
11:00	Bed

5:00 _____

5:30 _____

6:00 _____

6:30 _____

7:00 _____

7:30 _____

8:00 _____

8:30 _____

9:00 _____

9:30 _____

10:00 _____

10:30 _____

11:00 _____

11:30 _____

12:00 _____

12:30 _____

1:00 _____

1:30 _____

2:00 _____

2:30 _____

3:00 _____

3:30 _____

4:00 _____

4:30 _____

5:00 _____

5:30 _____

6:00 _____

6:30 _____

7:00 _____

7:30 _____

8:00 _____

8:30 _____

9:00 _____

9:30 _____

10:00 _____

10:30 _____

11:00 _____

11:30 _____

12:00 _____

12:30 _____

1:00 _____

1:30 _____

2:00 _____

2:30 _____

3:00 _____

❦

SEPTEMBER

Birthdays

_____

_____

_____

_____

_____

_____

_____

_____

_____

ACTIVITIES

Choose a Christ-like quality and practice it for a day. Write why you chose it and how it made you feel. Was it difficult? Easy? What did you learn about yourself?

Physical/Emotional Connection

Try this exercise during stressful or frustrating times. When music starts, shake your body for 3 minutes. (start with your head and move down to your feet). Then dance freely for 3 minutes. Notice how you felt during the shaking time. Notice how you felt while dancing freely. What did you learn about yourself?

What's Inside?

Stand in front of a mirror and say 'NO', softly, get louder and louder each time. Make faces and body gestures, as you repeat the word. Now, repeat the word 'Yes' in the same way. Describe what thoughts came up, how you felt, while saying each word.

Who am I?

Cut out magazine pics, describing what you think about yourself, and glue to a piece of paper.
On another sheet of paper, cut out and glue pictures showing how you want to feel.
On a third sheet of paper, draw or write how you are going to get from where you are now to where you want to be.

Valued and Worthy

Ask (3) people:
What are your greatest strengths, best qualities, and what you contribute to your relationship with them.

Journal Prompts

This is what happened…. I feel uncomfortable about….
I am happiest when… I can be creative by….
I am learning how to…. What I can do differently is…

Prayer

Our Father in heaven, Hallowed be your name, Your kingdom come your will be done, on Earth as it is in Heaven. Give us today our Daily Bread and Forgive us our debts, as we also have forgiven our debtors. And lead us not into temptation but deliver us from the evil one. *Mathew 6:9-*

Christ-Like Qualities

Loving	Trusting
Courageous	Peaceful
Surrendered	Creative
Compassion	Honest
Mindful	Humble
Accepting	Bold
Considerate	Grateful
Dependable	Confident
Discerning	Curious
Compassion	Patient
Considerate	Kind
Productive	Forgiving
Obedience	Faithful
Perseverant	Discipline
Temperate	Integrity
Authenticity	Courteous
Generous	Respectful
Responsible	Patient
Unchanging	Wise
Righteous	Eternal
Omnipotent	Sovereign

Armor of God

Helmet of SALVATION -NOTHING can separate you from God. *Romans 8:38-39*

Breastplate of RIGHTOUSNESS - ALL your sins are covered; you are purified. *1 John 1:7*

Shield of FAITH - He works ALL things for our good. *Romans 8:28*

Belt of TRUTH - God's word breathes life into your soul. *Hebrews 4:12*

Sword of the SPIRIT, word of God. Speak it OUTLOUD, to defeat the enemy. *Mathew 17:20*

Shoes of PEACE – *Philippians 4:7* and the READINESS to SERVE. *Luke 12:43*

Affirmation

I am a

_____,

_____,

_____

child of God.

*Choose three qualities, from Christ-like Qualities List, you would like to become or improve on. Speak aloud every day. Change anytime.

Memory Verse

_____

_____

_____

_____

_____

_____

Slow down....
Check your Choices & Responsibilities

Emotional IQ
Beliefs
Attitude
Intentions
Energy/Mood
Reactions/Responses
Actions/Behaviors
Decisions
Time

My Intention/Goal/Dream

_____

_____

_____

_____

_____

_____

_____

_____

Morning Mindset

1. Who is one person I can lift up/help today?

_____

_____

How?

_____

_____

2. One action, I can take, to-ward MY Intention, Goal, Dream(s) today Is…

_____

_____

_____

_____

3. What is the cost if I do not take the action(s)?

_____

_____

_____

_____

4. What can I intentionally learn today to support myself?

_____

_____

_____

5. What area of growth am I focusing on this week?

_____

_____

_____

Anti-Aging Face Regimen

Morning
Wash face w/cleanser
Vitamin C Serum
Hyaluronic Acid
Sunscreen SPF15

Noon
Sunscreen SPF15
Hyaluronic Acid
Toner (see Recipe)

B4 Bed
Wash Face
Alpha Hydroxy Acid
Retinol
Hyaluronic Acid
*Try a moisturizer w/
hyaluronic acid.

Toner Recipe

Harvest/Purchase
a handful of
Cell Rejuvenating Herb
(Lavender or Rose)
Place into 12oz. boiling
spring water, and
Let it sit overnight.
Strain and put into
spray bottle.

Breathe & Meditate

Take 5 minutes to Step away from everyone and everything.

Sit quietly. Once you have settled. (Record yourself or someone, in a monotone voice, saying…)

Think of the most serene place, of which you can think. Breathe Deep. In through your nose. Out through your mouth.

In this place, what is the weather like? Think of how it smells.

Think of how it feels.

What do you see?

Imagine Jesus is there.

He walks toward you.

Can you take his hand?

If not, you can follow him. You begin walking together.

As you walk, just breathe.

Now, open your eyes.

*Do this every morning and anytime you need comfort, strength, peace.
** IF you are unable to take Jesus' hand, keep practicing and it will get easier.

3) Daily Gratitude's

_____

_____

_____

Whole Health Cocktail
(drink 4oz. Every Morning)

2T Apple Cider Vinegar
4T Lemon Juice
2c. Cranberry Juice
4c. Water
Follow w/8oz. Bone broth

Raise Your Energy

- Stand and Bounce on your toes every hour.
- Swing your arms in circles
- Take Deep Breaths 10x.
- Brisk 5-minute Walk
- Listen to Uplifting Music
- Take a cold shower
- Take Vitamin B12
- Drink Ginseng tea

Exercise Tips

- Eat protein after working out or strenuous activities.
- Drink water in ounces equal to half your body weight.
- Make sure your sleep is consistent. *Setting your internal clock enables your body in its healing process.
- While working out call an accountability partner.

Fitness Routine
Weight/Height = BMI

Yoga	_____min
Walk	_____min
Aerobics	_____min
Swim	_____min
Cycle	_____min
Hike	_____min

Strength Training
Reps/weight#

Shoulders	___/___
Arms	___/___
Abs	___/___
Chest	___/___
Legs	___/___
Buttocks	___/___
Core	___/___

*Max heart rate = 220 less Your Age **Low rate = Max multiplied by .65.

Arms – Shoulder pinches and rolls, push-ups, butterflies, Curl ups and Back Rows

Legs – Squats, Step ups, Ball squeezes, Kick backs

Core – Planks and Leg lifts

Cleaning Routine
(See check list in back of book)

MUST Do

_____

Monday

_____
_____
_____

Tuesday

_____
_____
_____

NEED to Do

_____

Wednesday

_____
_____
_____

Thursday

_____
_____
_____

Friday

_____

WANT to DO

_____

Saturday

_____
_____
_____

Sunday

_____
_____
_____

Night Reflections

1. One thing I learned today.

_____

_____

_____

_____

2. What is one thing I can improve on/challenge myself.

_____

_____

_____

_____

_____

3. How am I eliminating distractions? Taking control of my time …

_____

_____

_____

_____

_____

4. What am I doing to improve my relationships?

_____

_____

_____

_____

_____

5. One question for God today: write it on separate piece of paper, put in a prayer box and leave with it for him.

Sample Routine
(Self Employed)

6:00	*Face/Prayer/Armor*
6:30	*Morning Cocktail &*
	Bone broth
7:00	*Breakfast/Bible Study*
7:30	
8:00	*Bounce & Breathe 10x*
8:30	
9:00	*Walk 15/Workout 15*
9:30	*Shower/Ready/*
	Affirmations
10:00	
10:30	*Cleaning (see routine)*
11:00	*Write*
11:30	
12:00	*Lunch – Meeting?*
12:30	*Write*
1:00	*Emails/Calls/Apt*
1:30	
2:00	
2:30	*Bounce/Breathe 10min*
3:00	*Write*
3:30	
4:00	*Craft/Garden/Visit*
4:30	
5:00	
5:30	
6:00	*Make Dinner/Go Out*
6:30	
7:00	*Eat dinner/Watch T.V.*
7:30	
8:00	*Clean up Dinner*
8:30	*Walk 15min*
9:00	*Pamper*
9:30	
10:00	*Facial/Ready for Bed*
10:30	*Night Reflections*
11:00	*Bed*

5:00 _____

5:30_____

6:00 _____

6:30 _____

7:00 _____

7:30 _____

8:00 _____

8:30 _____

9:00 _____

9:30 _____

10:00 _____

10:30 _____

11:00 _____

11:30 _____

12:00 _____

12:30 _____

1:00 _____

1:30 _____

2:00 _____

2:30 _____

3:00 _____

3:30 _____

4:00 _____

4:30 _____

5:00 _____

5:30 _____

6:00 _____

6:30 _____

7:00 _____

7:30 _____

8:00 _____

8:30 _____

9:00 _____

9:30 _____

10:00 _____

10:30 _____

11:00 _____

11:30 _____

12:00 _____

12:30 _____

1:00 _____

1:30 _____

2:00 _____

2:30 _____

3:00 _____

OCTOBER

Birthdays

_____

_____

_____

_____

_____

_____

_____

_____

_____

RELATIONSHIP WITH GOD

Many do not believe in the truth of God, because they were not taught or experiences, filtered through a 'lens' of hurt, betrayal, neglect, abuse, addictions, non-biblical teachings, etc....have caused people to distrust him. Distrusting God prevents us from receiving everything he wants for us. *And without faith it is impossible to please God because anyone who comes to him must believe that he exists and that he rewards those who earnestly seek him. Hebrew 11:6*

> What do you believe about God? What have you been taught? Do you have a relationship with him? Do you trust him? How much? With what?

God is the Creator - the Author of life. *Genesis 1:27*
God is Love. *1 John 4:16*
God is our Savior. *John 3:16*
God is our Provider. *Philippians 4:19*
God is our Teacher and Counselor. Psalms 32:8
God is our Healer. *Jeremiah 30:17*
God is a Triune God. 2 Corinthians 13:14

HEART STEPS

Believe he is – *John 3:16*
Confess your sins &
Ask forgiveness – *1 John 1:9*
Receive his love –*1 Corinthians 13*
Baptism of Holy Spirit –*Mark 16:16*
Build a Connection –*Ephesians 4:23-25*
Follow him – *Luke 9:23-24*
Church Fellowship – *1 John 1:6-7*
Practice Self-Control–*Galatians 5:22-23*
Bible Study – *2 Timothy 3:16*
Communicate w/Prayer –*Philippians 4:6*

God is Everywhere.
Proverbs 15:3
God is Powerful.
Mathew 19:26

Knowing information and feeling it in your heart can be difficult. But you can learn to trust God. Follow these "Heart Steps", to begin growing trust in your relationship with God.

Prayer

Our Father in heaven, Hallowed be your name, Your kingdom come your will be done, on Earth as it is in Heaven. Give us today our Daily Bread and Forgive us our debts, as we also have forgiven our debtors. And lead us not into temptation but deliver us from the evil one. *Mathew 6:9-*

Christ-Like Qualities

Loving	Trusting
Courageous	Peaceful
Surrendered	Creative
Compassion	Honest
Mindful	Humble
Accepting	Bold
Considerate	Grateful
Dependable	Confident
Discerning	Curious
Compassion	Patient
Considerate	Kind
Productive	Forgiving
Obedience	Faithful
Perseverant	Discipline
Temperate	Integrity
Authenticity	Courteous
Generous	Respectful
Responsible	Patient
Unchanging	Wise
Righteous	Eternal
Omnipotent	Sovereign

Armor of God

Helmet of
SALVATION -NOTHING can separate you from God.
Romans 8:38-39

Breastplate of
RIGHTOUSNESS - ALL your sins are covered; you are purified.
1 John 1:7

Shield of FAITH - He works ALL things for our good. *Romans 8:28*

Belt of TRUTH - God's word breathes life into your soul.
Hebrews 4:12

Sword of the SPIRIT, word of God. Speak it OUTLOUD, to defeat the enemy. *Mathew 17:20*

Shoes of PEACE – *Philippians 4:7* and the READINESS to SERVE.
Luke 12:43

Affirmation

I am a

_____,

_____,

_____

child of God.
*Choose three qualities, from Christ-like Qualities List, you would like to become or improve on. Speak aloud every day. Change anytime.

Memory Verse

_____

_____

_____

_____

_____

_____

Slow down....
Check your Choices &
Responsibilities

Emotional IQ

Beliefs

Attitude

Intentions

Energy/Mood

Reactions/Responses

Actions/Behaviors

Decisions

Time

My Intention/Goal/Dream

_____

_____

_____

_____

_____

_____

_____

_____

Morning Mindset

1. Who is one person I can lift up/help today?

_____

_____

How?

_____

_____

2. One action, I can take, to-ward MY Intention, Goal, Dream(s) today Is...

_____

_____

_____

_____

3. What is the cost if I do not take the action(s)?

_____

_____

_____

_____

4. What can I intentionally learn today to support myself?

_____

_____

_____

_____

5. What area of growth am I focusing on this week?

_____

_____

_____

Anti-Aging Face Regimen

Morning
Wash face w/cleanser
Vitamin C Serum
Hyaluronic Acid
Sunscreen SPF15

Noon
Sunscreen SPF15
Hyaluronic Acid
Toner (see Recipe)

B4 Bed
Wash Face
Alpha Hydroxy Acid
Retinol
Hyaluronic Acid
*Try a moisturizer w/
hyaluronic acid.

Toner Recipe

Harvest/Purchase
a handful of
Cell Rejuvenating Herb
(Lavender or Rose)
Place into 12oz. boiling
spring water, and
Let it sit overnight.
Strain and put into
spray bottle.

Breathe & Meditate

Take 5 minutes to Step away from everyone and everything.

Sit quietly. Once you have settled. (Record yourself or someone, in a monotone voice, saying…)

Think of the most serene place, of which you can think. Breathe Deep. In through your nose. Out through your mouth.

In this place, what is the weather like? Think of how it smells.

Think of how it feels.

What do you see?

Imagine Jesus is there.

He walks toward you.

Can you take his hand?

If not, you can follow him. You begin walking together.

As you walk, just breathe.

Now, open your eyes.

*Do this every morning and anytime you need comfort, strength, peace.
** IF you are unable to take Jesus' hand, keep practicing and it will get easier.

3) Daily Gratitude's

_____
_____
_____

Whole Health Cocktail

(drink 4oz. Every Morning)

2T Apple Cider Vinegar
4T Lemon Juice
2c. Cranberry Juice
4c. Water
Follow w/8oz. Bone broth

Raise Your Energy

- Stand and Bounce on your toes every hour.
- Swing your arms in circles
- Take Deep Breaths 10x.
- Brisk 5-minute Walk
- Listen to Uplifting Music
- Take a cold shower
- Take Vitamin B12
- Drink Ginseng tea

Exercise Tips

- Eat protein after working out or strenuous activities.
- Drink water in ounces equal to half your body weight.
- Make sure your sleep is consistent. *Setting your internal clock enables your body in its healing process.
- While working out call an accountability partner.

Fitness Routine

Weight/Height = BMI

Yoga	_____min
Walk	_____min
Aerobics	_____min
Swim	_____min
Cycle	_____min
Hike	_____min

Strength Training

Reps/weight#

Shoulders	____/____
Arms	____/____
Abs	____/____
Chest	____/____
Legs	____/____
Buttocks	____/____
Core	____/____

*Max heart rate = 220 less Your Age **Low rate = Max multiplied by .65.

Arms – Shoulder pinches and rolls, push-ups, butterflies, Curl ups and Back Rows

Legs – Squats, Step ups, Ball squeezes, Kick backs

Core – Planks and Leg lifts

Cleaning Routine

(See check list in back of book)

Monday

_____
_____
_____

Tuesday

_____
_____
_____

Wednesday

_____
_____
_____

Thursday

_____
_____
_____

Friday

_____
_____
_____

Saturday

_____
_____
_____

Sunday

_____
_____
_____

MUST Do

_____
_____
_____
_____

NEED to Do

_____
_____
_____
_____

WANT to DO

_____
_____
_____
_____

Night Reflections

1. One thing I learned today.

_____

_____

_____

_____

2. What is one thing I can improve on/challenge myself.

_____

_____

_____

_____

_____

3. How am I eliminating distractions? Taking control of my time …

_____

_____

_____

_____

4. What am I doing to improve my relationships?

_____

_____

_____

_____

_____

5. One question for God today: write it on separate piece of paper, put in a prayer box and leave with it for him.

Sample Routine
(Self Employed)

6:00	_Face/Prayer/Armor_
6:30	_Morning Cocktail &_
	Bone broth
7:00	_Breakfast/Bible Study_
7:30	
8:00	_Bounce & Breathe 10x_
8:30	
9:00	_Walk 15/Workout 15_
9:30	_Shower/Ready/_
	Affirmations
10:00	
10:30	_Cleaning (see routine)_
11:00	_Write_
11:30	
12:00	_Lunch – Meeting?_
12:30	_Write_
1:00	_Emails/Calls/Apt_
1:30	
2:00	
2:30	_Bounce/Breathe 10min_
3:00	_Write_
3:30	
4:00	_Craft/Garden/Visit_
4:30	
5:00	
5:30	
6:00	_Make Dinner/Go Out_
6:30	
7:00	_Eat dinner/Watch T.V._
7:30	
8:00	_Clean up Dinner_
8:30	_Walk 15min_
9:00	_Pamper_
9:30	
10:00	_Facial/Ready for Bed_
10:30	_Night Reflections_
11:00	_Bed_

Left	Right
5:00 _____	4:30 _____
5:30 _____	5:00 _____
6:00 _____	5:30 _____
6:30 _____	6:00 _____
7:00 _____	6:30 _____
7:30 _____	7:00 _____
8:00 _____	7:30 _____
8:30 _____	8:00 _____
9:00 _____	8:30 _____
9:30 _____	9:00 _____
10:00 _____	9:30 _____
10:30 _____	10:00 _____
11:00 _____	10:30 _____
11:30 _____	11:00 _____
12:00 _____	11:30 _____
12:30 _____	12:00 _____
1:00 _____	12:30 _____
1:30 _____	1:00 _____
2:00 _____	1:30 _____
2:30 _____	2:00 _____
3:00 _____	2:30 _____
3:30 _____	3:00 _____
4:00 _____	

NOVEMBER

Birthdays

_____

_____

_____

_____

_____

_____

_____

_____

_____

RELATIONSHIPS WITH SELF

When we are born, we are automatically dependent on our parents; looking to them for acceptance, security, and to provide our needs. Parents are then meant to teach their children to become independent. However, we get out into the world and are MADE to be dependent on others for: education, employment, housing, insurance, protection, food, etc. All of which depend entirely on **acceptance**. Many people who haven't been taught the skills needed to succeed become co-dependent on other 'worldly' things, to mask their feelings of fear, failure, ignorance, and confusion. This is not the vision the Lord had for us!

WE ARE DESIGNED TO BE CO-DEPENDENT ON GOD

I am the vine; you are the branches. If you remain in me and I in you; you will bear much fruit; apart from me <u>you can do nothing</u>. John 15:5

We are made in his image, a triune being, with a body, spirit, and soul! *Jesus replied, 'Love the Lord your God with all your heart, and with all your soul, and with all your mind and. With all your strength. Mark 12:30*

As Christians, we have all the power to do everything God calls us to do but, do you believe it? Do you believe you can do anything you set your mind to? Can you manage life's challenges? *And God is able to make all grace abound to you, so that having all sufficiency in all things at all times, you may abound in every good work. 2 Corinthians 9:8*

God expects us to be role models, replacing worldly thinking and behaviors, to be more Christ-like. *For you were once darkness, but now you are light in the Lord. Live as children of light. Ephesians 5:8*

Where is your C.A.B. taking you?	We are responsible for our: **C**ommunication **A**ctions **B**ehaviors

Prayer

Our Father in heaven, Hallowed be your name, Your kingdom come your will be done, on Earth as it is in Heaven. Give us today our Daily Bread and Forgive us our debts, as we also have forgiven our debtors. And lead us not into temptation but deliver us from the evil one. *Mathew 6:9-*

Christ-Like Qualities

Loving	Trusting
Courageous	Peaceful
Surrendered	Creative
Compassion	Honest
Mindful	Humble
Accepting	Bold
Considerate	Grateful
Dependable	Confident
Discerning	Curious
Compassion	Patient
Considerate	Kind
Productive	Forgiving
Obedience	Faithful
Perseverant	Discipline
Temperate	Integrity
Authenticity	Courteous
Generous	Respectful
Responsible	Patient
Unchanging	Wise
Righteous	Eternal
Omnipotent	Sovereign

Armor of God

Helmet of SALVATION -NOTHING can separate you from God. *Romans 8:38-39*

Breastplate of RIGHTOUSNESS - ALL your sins are covered; you are purified. *1 John 1:7*

Shield of FAITH - He works ALL things for our good. *Romans 8:28*

Belt of TRUTH - God's word breathes life into your soul. *Hebrews 4:12*

Sword of the SPIRIT, word of God. Speak it OUTLOUD, to defeat the enemy. *Mathew 17:20*

Shoes of PEACE – *Philippians 4:7* and the READINESS to SERVE. *Luke 12:43*

Affirmation

I am a

_____,

_____,

_____

child of God.

*Choose three qualities, from Christ-like Qualities List, you would like to become or improve on. Speak aloud every day. Change anytime.

Memory Verse

_____
_____
_____
_____
_____
_____
_____

Slow down....
Check your Choices &
Responsibilities

Emotional IQ
Beliefs
Attitude
Intentions
Energy/Mood
Reactions/Responses
Actions/Behaviors
Decisions
Time

My Intention/Goal/Dream

_____
_____
_____
_____
_____
_____
_____
_____
_____

Morning Mindset

1. Who is one person I can lift up/help today?

_____
_____

How?

_____
_____

2. One action, I can take, to-ward MY Intention, Goal, Dream(s) today Is…

_____
_____
_____
_____

3. What is the cost if I do not take the action(s)?

_____
_____
_____
_____

4. What can I intentionally learn today to support myself?

_____
_____
_____
_____

5. What area of growth am I focusing on this week?

_____
_____

Anti-Aging Face Regimen

Morning
Wash face w/cleanser
Vitamin C Serum
Hyaluronic Acid
Sunscreen SPF15

Noon
Sunscreen SPF15
Hyaluronic Acid
Toner (see Recipe)

B4 Bed
Wash Face
Alpha Hydroxy Acid
Retinol
Hyaluronic Acid
*Try a moisturizer w/
hyaluronic acid.

Toner Recipe

Harvest/Purchase

a handful of

Cell Rejuvenating Herb

(Lavender or Rose)

Place into 12oz. boiling
spring water, and

Let it sit overnight.

Strain and put into

spray bottle.

Breathe & Meditate

Take 5 minutes to Step away from everyone and everything.

Sit quietly. Once you have settled. (Record yourself or someone, in a monotone voice, saying...)

Think of the most serene place, of which you can think. Breathe Deep. In through your nose. Out through your mouth.

In this place, what is the weather like? Think of how it smells.

Think of how it feels.

What do you see?

Imagine Jesus is there.

He walks toward you.

Can you take his hand?

If not, you can follow him. You begin walking together.

As you walk, just breathe.

Now, open your eyes.

*Do this every morning and anytime you need comfort, strength, peace.
** IF you are unable to take Jesus' hand, keep practicing and it will get easier.

3) Daily Gratitude's

_____

_____

_____

Whole Health Cocktail

(drink 4oz. Every Morning)

2T Apple Cider Vinegar
4T Lemon Juice
2c. Cranberry Juice
4c. Water
Follow w/8oz. Bone broth

Raise Your Energy

- Stand and Bounce on your toes every hour.
- Swing your arms in circles
- Take Deep Breaths 10x.
- Brisk 5-minute Walk
- Listen to Uplifting Music
- Take a cold shower
- Take Vitamin B12
- Drink Ginseng tea

Exercise Tips

- Eat protein after working out or strenuous activities.
- Drink water in ounces equal to half your body weight.
- Make sure your sleep is consistent. *Setting your internal clock enables your body in its healing process.
- While working out call an accountability partner.

Fitness Routine

Weight/Height = BMI

Yoga	_____min
Walk	_____min
Aerobics	_____min
Swim	_____min
Cycle	_____min
Hike	_____min

Strength Training
Reps/weight#

Shoulders	___/___
Arms	___/___
Abs	___/___
Chest	___/___
Legs	___/___
Buttocks	___/___
Core	___/___

*Max heart rate = 220 less Your Age **Low rate = Max multiplied by .65.

Arms – Shoulder pinches and rolls, push-ups, butterflies, Curl ups and Back Rows

Legs – Squats, Step ups, Ball squeezes, Kick backs

Core – Planks and Leg lifts

Cleaning Routine
(See check list in back of book)

Monday

_____
_____
_____

Tuesday

_____
_____
_____

Wednesday

_____
_____
_____

Thursday

_____
_____
_____

Friday

_____
_____
_____

Saturday

_____
_____
_____

Sunday

_____
_____
_____

MUST Do

_____
_____
_____
_____

NEED to Do

_____
_____
_____
_____

WANT to DO

_____
_____
_____
_____

Night Reflections

1. One thing I learned today.

_____
_____
_____
_____

2. What is one thing I can improve on/challenge myself.

_____
_____
_____
_____
_____

3. How am I eliminating distractions? Taking control of my time …

_____
_____
_____
_____

4. What am I doing to improve my relationships?

_____
_____
_____
_____

5. One question for God today: write it on separate piece of paper, put in a prayer box and leave with it for him.

Sample Routine
(Self Employed)

6:00	Face/Prayer/Armor
6:30	Morning Cocktail & Bone broth
7:00	Breakfast/Bible Study
7:30	
8:00	Bounce & Breathe 10x
8:30	
9:00	Walk 15/Workout 15
9:30	Shower/Ready/ Affirmations
10:00	
10:30	Cleaning (see routine)
11:00	Write
11:30	
12:00	Lunch – Meeting?
12:30	Write
1:00	Emails/Calls/Apt
1:30	
2:00	
2:30	Bounce/Breathe 10min
3:00	Write
3:30	
4:00	Craft/Garden/Visit
4:30	
5:00	
5:30	
6:00	Make Dinner/Go Out
6:30	
7:00	Eat dinner/Watch T.V.
7:30	
8:00	Clean up Dinner
8:30	Walk 15min
9:00	Pamper
9:30	
10:00	Facial/Ready for Bed
10:30	Night Reflections
11:00	Bed

5:00 _____

5:30 _____

6:00 _____

6:30 _____

7:00 _____

7:30 _____

8:00 _____

8:30 _____

9:00 _____

9:30 _____

10:00 _____

10:30 _____

11:00 _____

11:30 _____

12:00 _____

12:30 _____

1:00 _____

1:30 _____

2:00 _____

2:30 _____

3:00 _____

3:30 _____

4:00 _____

4:30 _____

5:00 _____

5:30 _____

6:00 _____

6:30 _____

7:00 _____

7:30 _____

8:00 _____

8:30 _____

9:00 _____

9:30 _____

10:00 _____

10:30 _____

11:00 _____

11:30 _____

12:00 _____

12:30 _____

1:00 _____

1:30 _____

2:00 _____

2:30 _____

3:00 _____

DECEMBER

Birthdays

_____

_____

_____

_____

_____

_____

_____

_____

_____

HEALTHY RELATIONS
WITH OTHERS

Our thoughts, beliefs, communication, actions, and behaviors influence who we are, and that is the example we are setting for others. *Do your bet to present yourself to God as one approved; a worker who does not need to be ashamed and who correctly handles the word of truth. 2 Timothy 2:15*

God commands us **to Love** ourselves so, we can love others the same way. *'Love your neighbor, as yourself.' Mathew 22:39*

We are called to **be Humble**, when we are wrong, and responsible to admit it. *Therefore, confess your sins to each other so that you may be healed. The prayer of a righteous person is powerful and effective. James 5:16*

We are told to **Confront with Love;** when someone has wronged us, we are responsible to go to them and let them know so, they can make amends. *If your brother or sister sins, go and tell him his fault, just between the two of you.* Please read. *Mathew 18:15-17*

God tells us to **Forgive**. *Jesus said, "I tell you, not seven times but seventy-seven times." Mathew 18:22*

It is 'human nature' to feel betrayed, annoyed, aggravated, bitter, angry, depressed, insecure, etc.... However, the Lord gives us a way to overcome these feelings. The more we lean into him, worldly feelings are replaced with spiritual fruits, of compassion, mercy, grace, forgiveness, peace, etc. We learn to see others with spiritual eyes.

Many **Expectations** within our relationships are derived from our need to fulfill unmet needs. However, misconceptions in the world tell us, 'If it's not natural, it's not right.' 'Take me as I am or watch me walk away.' 'I shouldn't have to change for anybody.' 'If they don't do what I want, they don't love me.' 'If it's too hard, it's not meant to be." These are all lies! 'Healthy' relationships require work and dedication! AND they begin with trust.

Time – Recognition – Understanding - Security - Together

Time to build a **Connection.** Mindfulness, of others, is beneficial, when determining if a relationship is healthy for us; desired **Characteristics,** how they **Communicate,** are they **Consistent** in their communication, actions, and behaviors? *Come out from among them and be separate, says the Lord. Touch no unclean thing, and I will receive you.*
2 Corinthians 6:17

Recognition of how they are **Contributing** to the relationship; displays of understanding, compassion, support, service, encouragement, etc. OR drama, excuses, lies, manipulation, abuse, etc....Becoming aware of who you really are, what you really want, and who you are associating with is crucial to having healthy relationships. *Read Romans 8*

We look to others for **Understanding**, seeking validation, support, and encouragement, for our thoughts, behaviors, actions, and feelings. However, many <u>CAN NOT</u> understand. *But their minds were made dull, for to this day the same veil remains when the old covenant is read. It has not been re-moved, because only in Christ is it taken away. 2 Corinthians 3:14*

We also look to others and things for **Security**. However, this can only be obtained by knowing *The Lord himself goes before you and will be with you; he will never leave you nor forsake you. Do not be afraid; do not be discouraged. Deuteronomy 31:8*

The amount of time you spend **Together** determines how vulnerable you are. *Do not be misled; "Bad company corrupts good character." 1 Corinthians 15:33*

Prayer

Our Father in heaven, Hallowed be your name, Your kingdom come your will be done, on Earth as it is in Heaven. Give us today our Daily Bread and Forgive us our debts, as we also have forgiven our debtors. And lead us not into temptation but deliver us from the evil one. *Mathew 6:9-*

Christ-Like Qualities

Loving	Trusting
Courageous	Peaceful
Surrendered	Creative
Compassion	Honest
Mindful	Humble
Accepting	Bold
Considerate	Grateful
Dependable	Confident
Discerning	Curious
Compassion	Patient
Considerate	Kind
Productive	Forgiving
Obedience	Faithful
Perseverant	Discipline
Temperate	Integrity
Authenticity	Courteous
Generous	Respectful
Responsible	Patient
Unchanging	Wise
Righteous	Eternal
Omnipotent	Sovereign

Armor of God

Helmet of SALVATION -NOTHING can separate you from God. *Romans 8:38-39*

Breastplate of RIGHTOUSNESS - ALL your sins are covered; you are purified. *1 John 1:7*

Shield of FAITH - He works ALL things for our good. *Romans 8:28*

Belt of TRUTH - God's word breathes life into your soul. *Hebrews 4:12*

Sword of the SPIRIT, word of God. Speak it OUTLOUD, to defeat the enemy. *Mathew 17:20*

Shoes of PEACE – *Philippians 4:7* and the READINESS to SERVE. *Luke 12:43*

Affirmation

I am a

_____,

_____,

_____

child of God.

*Choose three qualities, from Christ-like Qualities List, you would like to become or improve on. Speak aloud every day. Change anytime.

Memory Verse

_____

_____

_____

_____

_____

_____

_____

Slow down....
**Check your Choices &
Responsibilities**

Emotional IQ
Beliefs
Attitude
Intentions
Energy/Mood
Reactions/Responses
Actions/Behaviors
Decisions
Time

My Intention/Goal/Dream

_____

_____

_____

_____

_____

_____

_____

_____

_____

Morning Mindset

1. Who is one person I can lift up/help today?

_____

_____

How?

_____

_____

2. One action, I can take, to-ward MY Intention, Goal, Dream(s) today Is…

_____

_____

_____

_____

3. What is the cost if I do not take the action(s)?

_____

_____

_____

_____

4. What can I intentionally learn today to support myself?

_____

_____

_____

_____

5. What area of growth am I focusing on this week?

_____

_____

_____

Anti-Aging Face Regimen

<u>Morning</u>
Wash face w/cleanser
Vitamin C Serum
Hyaluronic Acid
Sunscreen SPF15

<u>Noon</u>
Sunscreen SPF15
Hyaluronic Acid
Toner (see Recipe)

<u>B4 Bed</u>
Wash Face
Alpha Hydroxy Acid
Retinol
Hyaluronic Acid
*Try a moisturizer w/
hyaluronic acid.

Toner Recipe

Harvest/Purchase
a handful of
Cell Rejuvenating Herb
(Lavender or Rose)
Place into 12oz. boiling
spring water, and
Let it sit overnight.
Strain and put into
spray bottle.

Breathe & Meditate

Take 5 minutes to Step away from everyone and everything.

Sit quietly. Once you have settled. (Record yourself or someone, in a monotone voice, saying…)

Think of the most serene place, of which you can think. Breathe Deep. In through your nose. Out through your mouth.

In this place, what is the weather like? Think of how it smells.

Think of how it feels.

What do you see?

Imagine Jesus is there.

He walks toward you.

Can you take his hand?

If not, you can follow him. You begin walking together.

As you walk, just breathe.

Now, open your eyes.

*Do this every morning and anytime you need comfort, strength, peace.
** IF you are unable to take Jesus' hand, keep practicing and it will get easier.

3) Daily Gratitude's

_____

_____

_____

Whole Health Cocktail
(drink 4oz. Every Morning)

2T Apple Cider Vinegar
4T Lemon Juice
2c. Cranberry Juice
4c. Water
Follow w/8oz. Bone broth

Raise Your Energy

* Stand and Bounce on your toes every hour.
* Swing your arms in circles
* Take Deep Breaths 10x.
* Brisk 5-minute Walk
* Listen to Uplifting Music
* Take a cold shower
* Take Vitamin B12
* Drink Ginseng tea

Exercise Tips

* Eat protein after working out or strenuous activities.
* Drink water in ounces equal to half your body weight.
* Make sure your sleep is consistent. *Setting your internal clock enables your body in its healing process.
* While working out call an accountability partner.

Fitness Routine
Weight/Height = BMI

Yoga	____min
Walk	____min
Aerobics	____min
Swim	____min
Cycle	____min
Hike	____min

Strength Training
Reps/weight#

Shoulders	___/___
Arms	___/___
Abs	___/___
Chest	___/___
Legs	___/___
Buttocks	___/___
Core	___/___

*Max heart rate = 220 less Your Age **Low rate = Max multiplied by .65.

Arms – Shoulder pinches and rolls, push-ups, butterflies, Curl ups and Back Rows

Legs – Squats, Step ups, Ball squeezes, Kick backs

Core – Planks and Leg lifts

Cleaning Routine
(See check list in back of book)

MUST Do

_____

Monday

_____

_____

_____

_____

Tuesday

_____

_____

_____

NEED to Do

Wednesday

_____

_____

_____

_____

Thursday

_____

_____

_____

_____

Friday

_____

_____

WANT to DO

_____

Saturday

_____

_____

_____

_____

Sunday

_____

_____

_____

_____

Night Reflections

1. One thing I learned today.

_____
_____
_____
_____

2. What is one thing I can improve on/challenge myself.

_____
_____
_____
_____
_____

3. How am I eliminating distractions? Taking control of my time …

_____
_____
_____
_____

4. What am I doing to improve my relationships?

_____
_____
_____
_____
_____

5. One question for God today: write it on separate piece of paper, put in a prayer box and leave with it for him.

Sample Routine
(Self Employed)

6:00	Face/Prayer/Armor
6:30	Morning Cocktail & Bone broth
7:00	Breakfast/Bible Study
7:30	
8:00	Bounce & Breathe 10x
8:30	
9:00	Walk 15/Workout 15
9:30	Shower/Ready/Affirmations
10:00	
10:30	Cleaning (see routine)
11:00	Write
11:30	
12:00	Lunch – Meeting?
12:30	Write
1:00	Emails/Calls/Apt
1:30	
2:00	
2:30	Bounce/Breathe 10min
3:00	Write
3:30	
4:00	Craft/Garden/Visit
4:30	
5:00	
5:30	
6:00	Make Dinner/Go Out
6:30	
7:00	Eat dinner/Watch T.V.
7:30	
8:00	Clean up Dinner
8:30	Walk 15min
9:00	Pamper
9:30	
10:00	Facial/Ready for Bed
10:30	Night Reflections
11:00	Bed

5:00 _____	4:30 _____
5:30_____	5:00 _____
6:00 _____	5:30 _____
6:30 _____	6:00 _____
7:00 _____	6:30 _____
7:30 _____	7:00 _____
8:00 _____	7:30 _____
8:30 _____	8:00 _____
9:00 _____	8:30 _____
9:30 _____	9:00 _____
10:00 _____	9:30 _____
10:30 _____	10:00 _____
11:00 _____	10:30 _____
11:30 _____	11:00 _____
12:00 _____	11:30 _____
12:30 _____	12:00 _____
1:00 _____	12:30 _____
1:30 _____	1:00 _____
2:00 _____	1:30 _____
2:30 _____	2:00 _____
3:00 _____	2:30 _____
3:30 _____	3:00 _____
4:00 _____	

HEALTHY PANTRY STAPLES

Veggies	**Fruits**	**Meats**	**Spices**
Lettuce	Lemons	80/20 Beef	Cinnamon
Spinach	Limes	Chicken	Garlic
Brussels	Oranges	Tuna	Ginger
Squash	Grapefruit	Salmon	Turmeric
Onions	Watermelon	Cod	Cumin
Cabbage	Apples	T-bone	Curry
Celery	Pears	Eggs	Paprika
Zucchini	Strawberries		Sage
Swiss Chard	Raspberries	**Healthy Fats**	Cayenne
Green Beans	Blueberries	Butter	Rosemary
Broccoli	Mulberries	Black Olives	Basil
Cauliflower	Blackberries	Avocado	Chives
Squash	Kiwi	Olive Oil	Thyme
Pumpkin	Bananas	Coconut Oil	Marjoram
Cucumber	Pineapple	Hemp Seeds	Oregano
Romaine	Grapes	Flax Seeds	Cilantro
Avocado	Papaya		Monk Fruit
Kale	Mango	**Grains**	**Saffron**
Peppers	Peaches	Quinoa	Fennel seed
Asparagus	Melons	Brown Rice	Cardamom
Mushrooms		Oats	Nutmeg
Carrots	**Roots**	Barley	Anise
Celery	Ginger		Clove
Tomatoes	Horseradish	**Condiments**	
Fennel	Red Potato	Worcestershire	
	Sweet. Potato	Liquid Aminos	
	Turnip	Siracha	
	Radish	Mustard	
	Yucca	Vinegar	
	Kali Rabi	Salsa	
		ACV	

WHOLE HOUSE

Daily
Wash, Dry & Fold (1) load
Take Out Trash

Weekly
Mop and Polish floors
Dust light fixtures, blinds,
Doors, Baseboards, and
Doorframes

Seasonally
Change lightbulbs
Change Air filters
Change Batteries in Detectors
Wash Windows

Yearly
Steam Clean Carpets
Check Freezer Expirations
Clean inside Cabinets

BATHROOM

Daily
Pick up Clothes
Clean sink counter

Weekly
Clean Toilet
Clean Tub & Shower
Clean Mirrors

Monthly
Clean Shower Curtain
Wash Rugs

Yearly
Clean Cabinets

LIVING ROOM

Daily
Pick up misc.

Weekly
Vacuum/Sweep & Dust Mop
Dust Tables & Cabinets
Dust Electronics & Pictures

Seasonally
Wash Throw Pillows & Blankets

KITCHEN

Daily
Dishes (wash & put away)
Wipe down Counters
Empty Trash

Weekly
Sweep & Mop Floors
Expired Food in Fridge
Scrub Sink
Clean Microwave
Clean Stove top
Clean out Fridge
Clean small Appliances
Wash out garbage can

Seasonally
Clean Garbage Disposal
Clean Oven

Yearly
Clean top of Cabinets

BEDROOMS

Daily
Make Bed
Pick up Clothes & Shoes

Weekly
Wash Bedding
Vacuum/Sweep & Dust mop
Dust Dressers & Pictures
Clean Mirrors
Take clothes to Dry Cleaners

Seasonally
Flip & Rotate Mattress

Yearly
Vacuum Drapes/Clean Blinds
Clean Curtains
Unwanted Clothes to Charity

LAUNDRY ROOM

Daily
Clean Dryer Lint

Weekly
Sweep & Dust Mop
Wipe down Washer/Dryer
Empty Trash

Seasonally
Run Cleaning Cycle
Clean Dryer Duct

GARAGE

Daily
Put away Tools as Used

Weekly
Sweep Floors & Pick up
Clean out Vehicles
Take out Trash

Yearly
Organize Sporting Equipment,
Tools, Toys, Seasonal Decor

OFFICE

Daily
Back up/Delete files

Weekly
File important Documents
Refill Office Supplies
Dust Desktop & Electronics

CLEANING TIPS

- Peroxide on blood stains
- Baking soda for burnt food on pots
- Charcoal to rid musty smells
- Put dryer sheets in vents for fragrance throughout your house
- Use Goo Gone for removing stickers and labels

SELF-DISCOVERY QUESTIONNAIRE

Your Strengths

1. What were your favorite subjects in school?
2. What do you yearn to do?
3. What do you get complimented on most?
4. What do you like doing?
5. What are you passionate about? What causes you to lose track of time?
6. What are you proud of?
7. What experiences have you had that cause you to feel unique?
8. What skills and/or talents do you have?
9. What brings you joy? What is the happiest you have been?
10. What are your best character qualities?
11. What is the first thing you think about in the morning? How do you spend the first five minutes of your day?
12. What are you grateful for?

How you Relate w/Others

1. Do others in your life support you? Can you ask for help? Who can you ask for help?
2. How much of your time revolves around others? How much do others depend on you? How much do you depend on others?
3. Do you have set boundaries or limits with the people in your life?
4. What do you do when your boundaries have been crossed?
5. How do you communicate what you need, want, believe?
6. How do you discuss what you do not want, do not like, or do not agree with?
7. What expectations do you have for people in your life?
8. How do you get along with your coworkers? Do you work well with others? Do you take your work home?
9. Do you feel comfortable in your home? Do you feel safe? Do you feel free to be yourself?
10. What Christ-like characters are you promoting?

Concerning your Past

1. How much time do you spend thinking about the past?
2. What difficulties have you overcome?
3. Are there unresolved issues? Do you feel shame, anger, bitterness, etc.?
4. Do you know of anyone you need to ask forgiveness? Do you know anyone you need to forgive?
5. What upsets you (your triggers)? What causes you to feel anxiety, frustrated, angry, sad?
6. Are you in control of your emotions or are they controlling you?
7. Do you have a lot of clutter in your home? Do you have things stuffed and/or piled in corners, closets, garage?
8. What defense mechanisms have you been using? Are they still beneficial or can you use a new coping skill?
9. Can you recognize people who do not have good intentions? What characteristics do they demonstrate?
10. Is your love conditional or unconditional? Think on each person as you encounter them.
11. What has been keeping you from acting on things you know you need to do?

Self-Care

1. What does a healthy lifestyle look like to you?
2. What is your relationship with food? Do you eat when your body tells you to or wait until you get 'hangry'?
3. Are your meals scheduled? How much do of your diet is fast food? How much of your food intake is processed?
4. How much sugar do you eat? How much fat does your diet contain? Do you eat vegetables?
5. What is your energy level?
6. Do you exercise regularly? How often do you take a walk?
7. Do you have quiet space to reflect and hold your thoughts captive?
8. Do you go to the doctor when needed?
9. Do you pamper yourself? Moisturize your body; do your nails, hair; give yourself a facial?

Planning Ahead

1. What do you want your life to look like? What are you doing? Who are you doing it with? Where are you? When would you like to do it? What steps would you need to take to do that?
2. What values and morals do you want to demonstrate?
3. What are you passionate about?
4. How do/will you hold yourself accountable and motivated?
5. What boundaries are you setting?
6. How will you spend your free time to benefit yourself and those around you?
7. What goals are you setting for yourself? What are the steps needed to do that?
8. How will you demonstrate my walk with Christ?
9. How can you consistently stay confident in your identity in Christ?
10. What skills do you need to develop to do the things you want?
11. What idols are you letting go of?
12. How will you respond when you are triggered? When someone reacts negatively, how will you respond?

Journal Starters

What is keeping me from...

What is the opposite of ....

What needs to happen in order for me to become clear on.....................

I am letting go of....................................because..................................

What thoughts would I have to think, in order to feel................

I am open to changing my.....................because...................................

I can choose..because ....

What would my best self-do in this situation ....

What does this mean to me..

I felt...when ....

What I want more than anything is ....

What steps do I need to take before I can ....

When I am feeling....................................I can ....

When I recognize I am trying to control outcomes, I will......................

Printed in the United States
by Baker & Taylor Publisher Services